PRACTICAL
DEMONSTRATIONS

of the

ANOINTING
SECOND EDITION

FREQUENCY REVELATOR

Global Destiny Publishing
House (Pty) Ltd

Published by the Author © Global Destiny Publishing House, Sandton, South Africa

Website: www.globaldestinypublishers.com

Email: frequency.revelator@gmail.com

Phone: 0027622436745/ 0027785416006/0027797921646

Book layout and cover designed by Frequency Revelator for Global Destiny Publishing House

Divine Rights and Privileges of a Believer

Keys to Unlocking the Supernatural

The Dynamics of God's Word

7 Supernatural Dimensions of Financial Prosperity

Spiritual Laws and Principles of the Kingdom

Rain of Revelations Daily Devotional Concordance

Practical Demonstrations of the Anointing

Understanding Times And Seasons In God's Calendar

How To Defeat The Spirit Of Witchcraft

The Practice Of God's Presence

21 Ways Of How To Hear God's Voice Clearly

How To Activate And Fully Exercise The Gifts Of The Spirit

Jehovah Yahweh: Understanding The Different Names of God

The Prophetic Significance Of Gold Dust Silver Stones,

Diamonds And Other Precious Stones

Deeper Revelations Of The Five-Fold Ministry

The Anatomy And Physiology Of The Anointing

Understanding Prophetic Dreams And Visions

Deeper Revelations Of The Glory Realm

The Power Of The Apostolic Anointing

The Anointing, The Mantle & The Glory

The Power of Speaking In Tongues

Miracles, Signs And Wonders

Resurrection Power

The Essence of Worship

Rain of Fire

Healing Rains

The Realm Of Love

The Revelation Of Jesus Christ

The Second Coming Of Jesus Christ

CONTENT

AKNOWLEDGEMENTS

This Second Topical compendium on the Anointing is primarily dedicated to the Holy Ghost, who is the author and the finisher of the deep revelations encapsulated in this publication. There is no book in any Christian Library on the subject of the anointing which is as deep and comprehensive as this publication. This insightful, refreshing, profound and biblically sound revelation awakens the believer to the reality of how the anointing of God can be practically demonstrated in any setting whether it's at school, church, home, office or anywhere else. It is chiefly the Holy Ghost who trained me in matters of operating in the realm of the anointing. He has proven to me that when I practically demonstrate the anointing of God, it is actually Him who does the work, hence it is my passion that the reader will see Him throughout the pages of this book and not any man.

I would like to express my deep and unparalleled gratitude to the Generals who are striding at the frontline in the practical demonstration of the anointing of the Holy Spirit; namely, Pastor Benny Hinn of the World Healing Centre Church, Pastor Chris the President of the Believers' Love World International Ministry and Dr. Peter Tan of Eagle Vision Ministry. These men of God have immensely coached me in the direction of moving and operating in the anointing of the Holy Spirit. Dr Peter Tan is one man of God who truly made a difference in my life, for it was under his tutelage that I developed an insatiable appetite and perennial hunger to practically demonstrate the *anointing* and thus, became interested in the practical demonstration of God's power than just preaching about it.

Most preachers *talk about the anointing* and God's power but *very few hardly demonstrate it,* but Dr Peter Tan challenged me not just to talk about God's word but to practically demonstrate it and produce the results of what it talks about, hence, he became more of a mentor to me than just a minister of the gospel.

Frequency Revelator

I would like to extend my gratitude to my ministry partners for creating a conducive platform and spiritual climate for me to move in greater depths, higher realms and deeper dimensions of the anointing, to shake the nations and touch multitudes around the globe. It is for such a reason that I have been used by God as a vehicle to propagate the new waves of God's anointing to the furthest territories across the globe, to accomplish His divine plans at such a time as this. My thanks also goes to Author House (UK), for making my dream of writing a reality by publishing the first edition of this book, thereby enabling me to fulfil God's dream of propagating the world with revelations of God's word.

I would like to extend a hand of appreciation to Maryna De Canha for her relentless support and professional guidance in my career. Thanks to Pastor Moses Vhikey my Director for Resurrection Embassy, my Marketing Director for Kingdom Millionaires Global Investments (KMGI) (Pty) Ltd, Pastor Gabriel Coke, Pastor Patson May, Pastor Victor, Prophet Ron, and Dr. Franklin Ndhlovu. Further thanks goes to all my siblings for their love and support in every way. Thanks to my ministry partners and television viewers, for being so instrumental in my life in birthing the vision God has bestowed upon my life. I command the blessings of the Lord to abundantly marinate every sphere of your life with the rain of the anointing in Jesus' Name!

-Apostle Frequency Revelator

CHAPTER ONE

PRACTICAL DEMONSTRATIONS OF THE ANOINTING

A Presentation of Comprehensive Practical Guidelines To Demonstrating The Anointing

It is of paramount significance to highlight right from the onset the divine truth that the anointing is not just a theoretical concept; instead it is a practical divine phenomenon that can be demonstrated practically to impact the lives of multitudes across the globe. The anointing is not a hazy, mysterious phenomenon that people should just preach, rant and rave about; instead it is a tangible spiritual substance which can be transmuted from the spirit realm into a visible form in the natural in such a way that people can see it, touch it and use it. Therefore, anybody who *talks about the anointing* instead of *talking the anointing* grossly compromises the standard which heaven has ordained for operating in the anointing. There is a difference between *talking about the anointing* and *talking the anointing*. The former infers a provision of theoretical or theological perspective to the subject of the anointing while the latter implies a practical demonstration of this divine phenomenon. However, it is an optimum integration of both the theoretical and practical perspectives that breeds tremendous results of power when operating or moving in the *anointing*.

Therefore, in this section, an attempt has been made to integrate the word of God with my personal spiritual experiences and encounters in the anointing so as to reinforce an understanding of this divine phenomenon. The subject of anointing is thus holistically approached from both a *theoretical* and *practical perspectives*. Demonstrations of the anointing through the use of physical instruments or objects, body parts, gestures, clothes and other

10

living or non-living items are presented in this writing. A detailed description of each type of anointing is accompanied by a practical illustration or demonstration in an endeavour to establish the authenticity of the concept and enhance a deeper understanding of the subject of *the anointing*. These are divergent types of anointing which God used me to demonstrate in the course of my ministry, hence this publication is meant to supplement the theoretical evidence, thereby enhancing further understanding of the above teaching on *the anointing*. It should be understood in this regard that these different types of the anointing and their terminology depend on the nature of its flow, operation and how it is being administered, hence must not be taken as a religious doctrine but a means to learning *new things in the anointing*.

In this last dispensation, these types of anointing that the Holy Spirit is revealing shall become a common occurrence for the chosen vessels that the Lord is preparing and raising up in secret. The only thing that can hinder you from flowing in such anointing will be the man-inspired teachings and doctrines of your past. The devil will use the wrong teachings implanted in your mind as certification to block these types of anointing from flowing in your life and ministry. At times, the Holy Spirit might take time to undo the wrong teachings in your mind and heart depending on the degree of yieldedness to Him. If you do not give time to the Holy Spirit to teach you now, your mind and heart will be a major block to these new types of anointing that the Holy Spirit has prepared for the end times. The second blockage to the anointing could be sin in your life. The third is when you are not prepared properly and spiritually. The fourth blockage could be an external one and might come from your loved ones, like your spouses. The fifth blockage could be wrong attitudes in your spirit and it is not easy for the Holy Spirit to undo them if you are not willing to change. The devil will bombard you by reminding you of this scripture and that scripture and this teaching and that teaching in order to prevent these new types of anointing to flow in your life. If you do not have the Holy Spirit to reveal to you the truth about these scriptures and teachings, the twisted interpretation and deception given by the devil and his agents will hinder you.

DIVERGENT TYPES OF ANOINTINGS

A Divine Revelation of **100** *Different Types of Anointings And Their Practical Application*

1. THE OVERFLOW ANOINTING OR RUN-OFF ANOINTING

This is a *measureless anointing* that by character and nature of manifestation overflows like a heavy rain when released to touch multitudes of people in a particular territory. This is the highest level of manifestation of the anointing. One distinctive feature of the overflow anointing is that when in manifestation, it cannot be contained, or measured; it cannot be controlled, interrupted, regulated or predicted. It manifests itself like a food of running waters such that its flow and movement cannot be stopped, influenced, controlled or manipulated in any way. It's like God pouring Himself abundantly and uninterruptedly upon His people. In other words, it is a reflection of a display of God's supremacy and sovereign power over His creation. When God declared in Ephesians 3:20 that *I will do exceedingly and abundantly beyond what you think or ask,* He actually spoke about the *overflow anointing and blessings* which He shall release upon His people. In other words, it is so abundant and copious such that it exceeds the expectations of its recipients by manifesting even without asking or thinking about it.

The character of its manifestation is such that when released in a particular place, it flows and runs through the congregation like a flood of heavy rain. It overflows and touches even people, areas or places further than its scope of operation and sphere of influence. In other words, it overflows or overlaps to invade newer, uncommon and hidden territories. That is why it is called an *overflow anointing*. When the bible says that Jesus had a spirit without measure (John 3:34), it actually refers to this type of anointing. In other words, Jesus constantly, profusely and perennially operated and moved in the realm of *the overflow or measureless anointing* to the extent that it is recorded in Mathew 12:15 *that He healed every one of the sick that were brought to him*. This implies that it takes an unprecedented *overflow anointing* to anoint or heal everyone in the auditorium because this kind of anointing doesn't have limitations, restrictions or boundaries. The good news is that we have the same measure of anointing which Jesus operated under during His earthly ministry, hence we can tap and flow in the same dimension of the *overflow anointing*.

To substantiate this revelation with further scriptural evidence, it is recorded in Acts 10:1 that when Peter was invited to preach at Cornelius's house, the instant he began to speak, *the Holy Ghost fell upon ALL them that heard the word*. In the context of this revelation, the phrase *fell"* describes the character of manifestation of the anointing that was released at that place. In other words, the anointing overflowed to touch everybody as long as they heard the word. That means even those who were not present in the meeting but overhead the word being preached also received a doze of that anointing. This is to tell you that Peter moved in the realm of the *overflow anointing* to provoke the perennial and heavy torrential downpour of God's power. Unlike other types of anointing, the overflow anointing does not need *channelling* because it flows uninterruptedly even without the minister doing anything. The Holy Ghost is the one who determines the direction of this anointing, hence the duty of the minister is simply to cooperate with Him and channel it appropriately.

To cement this revelation with practical evidence, I have read about how John G. Lake an anointed man of God ministered in Johannesburg in the early 1950s and the anointing was so much that even a week after he had left the place the anointing was still overflowing and hitting the masses on the streets. In other words, after ministering in South Africa even two week after John G. Lake had left the city, the anointing was so strong that it engulfed the whole atmosphere such that people were falling under the power in the streets and market places long after he had gone, even without ushers, a choir or a preaching. In other words, people were still hit by the anointing and falling under the power in the streets where there was no church service going on. This is the character of manifestation of the *overflow anointing*. This type of anointing is not only limited to people's bodies but once released in a particular territory, it lingers in the atmosphere, on buildings, walls, floor, trees and virtually on every object such that it begins to create an atmosphere of its own in that territory. It knows no boundary; it has no jurisdiction or limitations. If a minister intends to anoint the whole congregation, this is the type of anointing that he should tap into. Its impact is felt right across a broad spectrum of location both geographically and spiritually. In other words, it has far reaching geographical and spiritual effects. It has the longest life span and can even persist or linger on buildings, foliage and in air even long after its ministration has ended. Moreover, it is written about the renowned revivalist Charles Finney that whenever he used to visit a town or city, the people would sense the anointing so strongly that they would automatically repent and cry for mercy under the conviction of the Holy Spirit. Not once did Finney pray for that kind of anointing, instead he pursued God to give him the perishing souls. I have also heard of Maria Woodworth Etter, a great woman of God who moved so much in the anointing such that the people would be touched by the power of God to the extent of falling under the power while she was still approaching the church about two kilometres away.

In Ezekiel 47:3, Ezekiel speaks of the overflow anointing when he presents a narrative about a man with a measuring line who measured the waters, which flow in the temple which depict different levels, depths and dimensions in the realm of the anointing. According to Ezekiel, at first as the man with a measuring line measured the waters, and the water came to the ankles, and as he continued, the water was brought up to the ankles, then knees, then waste and the water level kept on accumulating until it reached the level of the *overflow anointing* described as a river in flood. It's like a flood of waters; it's like a torrential downpour of heavy rain. Once it has been released in a particular territory, regardless of the people's conductivity and expectancy levels, it breaks out like the breakthrough of waters and touches everybody such that it is impossible for one to be a spectator in the place where the anointing is flowing. Because of the gravity, intensity and veracity of its manifestation, as well as its ability to change the spiritual atmosphere of a territory, at times it's advisable just to channel and release this anointing into the atmosphere rather than upon individuals. The gravest mistake which a minister can make is to lay hands on people when this anointing is in manifestation. Instead, just speak the word and channel it in the direction of your words.

The overflow anointing is usually poured by the Holy Ghost when He wants to ignite a revival over a city, town or nation. This is the same dimension or effulgence of the anointing that rained and overflowed at Pentecost (Acts 2:1) and gave the disciples in the Upper Room extraordinary boldness such that they burst forth into the marketplace, filled with the power of God and impacted the nations and manifested God's power in a global arena. How do I know that this was an overflow anointing? It's because of the character of its manifestation. This was an overdose of the anointing because it was not the first time the believers received the anointing. However, the way it manifested or the magnitude, gravity and intensity of its manifestation is what made a difference. Some folks in the Old Testament had received the anointing but we don't see them behaving this way. What it means is that the anointing had overflowed in greater measure. In other words, it was increased beyond measure and was now engulfing and invading even the spiritual atmosphere, causing these ordinary men to burst forth into the public arena to take centre stage of the world.

Moreover, when the bible gives a description in Psalms 133:1 of *how pleasant it is for brethren to gather together in unity* and it further elucidates by giving a figurative illustration that *it is like oil poured on the head of Aaron, running down his beads*, it actually speaks of the *overflow anointing*. In the same way oil runs down the beads, to the extent that the whole body becomes drenched in the anointing, the overflow anointing naturally flows and oozes through every fibre of your being, it runs over your body like a stream of rain. In other words, it flows through every fibre of your being and infiltrates the core of your being; it flows and ignites fire in your bones, it oozes through your marrow, and invades even the cells in your blood, driving out devils and birthing forth a healing process. David concurs with this revelation, hence he proclaimed in Psalms 23:25, *you anoint my head with oil, my cup runs over.* This speaks of the *overflow anointing.* Any man who operates in this dimension of the anointing will instantaneously be catapulted into a higher realm of glory.

Practical demonstration

I recall vividly my first meeting when I was invited to preach at Campus Ministry at my University. That evening, I was so saturated with high volumes of divine energy to the extent that the instant I stepped on the stage as to minister on the anointing, as I unveiled the revelations of God's word, under the sound of my voice, the Holy Ghost fell on the congregation, provoking an uninterrupted flow and a heavy torrential downpour of the anointing over the congregation. It was as if I had literally stepped into the dimension which Peter tapped into at Cornelius house in (Acts 10:1). It seemed like a mighty whirlwind came into the Auditorium and instantly hundreds of people in the congregation started falling all over the place under the power of the Holy Spirit by themselves as the wind of God blew in that place. As a thick visible cloud was seen hanging over the atmosphere, no one could withstand the weight of God's glory that enveloped that auditorium.

15

As I took a prophetic step to release the atmosphere in that place, multitudes of those who came into contact with my shadow, fell under the power like apples falling from a tree. As if that was not enough, as I was passing by walking down the aisle, I heard a loud noise behind me, and when I turned around to look, almost all the choir, ushers and even those who were assisting me were also under the power of God. As the anointing intensified and engulfed the whole atmosphere, I was barely able to stand as the presence of God consumed me and before long, I eventually succumbed to the power of God and was also slain in Spirit. When I fully regained my consciousness, there were piles of bodies lying unceremoniously all over the auditorium, with shirts wrinkled and ties askew as if it were a slaughter house. Bodies were strewn across the floor as if gangsters had stepped into the auditorium with machine guns and mowed people down in their tracks, shirts wrinkled and ties askew. Ladies hair-dos, so carefully brushed and sprayed, had been lost to the experience of collapsing in the power of the Spirit on the floor. There was no semblance of sophistication anywhere as multitudes lay on their faces or backs, stacked in aisles and walkways throughout the auditorium.

One striking experience is that in the midst of that chaotic situation, deep, incessant spiritual cries, prayers and worship were arising simultaneously from all sides of the congregation as the masses were uncontrollably basking under the reverence of the glory of God. Mixed sounds of laughter, exhilaration and weeping mingled with quiet music flowing from a sound system echoed through the auditorium. It was a long, long time before the natural order came back to the church and everyone left one by one greatly touched by the presence of God. As a result of that wave of the Spirit, a multitude of people had supernatural encounters, individual peculiarities and divergent manifestations and the impact of that meeting continues to last in the lives of those who were present. Philosophically speaking, there is an unmistakable imprint of the Divine stamped on the life of every one who was touched by that unusual manifestation of God's anointing. That was indeed an invasion of God's glory ! That presence was so thick, sacred and unusual such that if someone had brought a dead person in a coffin, he would have rose instantly without anybody laying hands on him. Many miracles took place that day and that heavy, torrential downpour of the anointing and God's power never stopped flowing into my life until today.

2. SPILL OVER ANOINTING

This is a spontaneous kind of anointing that spills over from the minister into the congregation as they listen to the preaching of the word. Depending on the level of conductivity and receptivity levels, some believers are able to absorb the anointing directly from a minister even without talking, touching or saying anything to him or placing a demand. Instead, just by sitting in an environment or place where the spiritual atmosphere of the anointing has been cultivated, members of the congregation can absorb the anointing directly from the minister. In other words, it works through *impartation* and *placing a demand* on the mantle upon an anointed man of God. In these modern days where technology is advanced, it is possible for one to absorb an anointing by watching television, reading anointed books, listening to DVDs, listening to worship music and so forth. The scriptural basis of the *spill over anointing* is found in Acts 10:1 where by the anointing started flowing upon the people the instant Peter spoke the word of God in Cornelius's house. However, the major difference between the *spill over anointing* and *overflow anointing* is that the spill over anointing does not rain from heaven upon the masses. Instead, it flows from the minister to the congregation as God uses the spirit of the minister as an arch or vehicle to touch his people. Its manifestation is dependent on the word that is being preached, hence it flows for a moment and weans or is lifted immediately after the word is ministered. Its manifestation is also dependent on the proximity or relationship between the minister and the believer, hence if the relationship is cut off, the anointing is also lifted.

With this kind of anointing, it is not necessary for one to make an outer call as is the norm in many churches. Instead, the congregation gets to absorb this anointing concurrently as the word is ministered. Remember that God watches over His word to perform it. As the word is preached, the Holy Spirit acts on it by realising the flow of the anointing which spills over from the minister to the crowd. This is why some people start to cry or tremble or fall under the power even when the minister is still preaching the word. Many even receive miracles of healing, deliverance and breakthrough while the minister is still preaching the word. When this type of anointing flows, there is no need to make outer calls as is tendency in many churches because everyone in the congregation gets to be soaked under the anointing.

This type of anointing does not need laying of hands as is the norm during impartation. Instead, by sitting in the congregation where an anointed minister is teaching the word, one can literally absorb the anointing that is flowing through him. This is because God uses the human spirit of a minister to touch the congregation, hence as the anointing flows into his spirit and floods it, it also flows out to flood the spirits of those in the congregation. In other words, there is an *"inflow"* and *"outflow"* of the anointing in and out of the human vessel. It is called a *spill over anointing* because it spills over from the spirit of the minister into the spirit of those listening to him in the congregation in the same way water spills over from a lake into a river. Through this kind of anointing, it becomes easier for a person sitting on the congregation to place a demand on the anointing upon the minister and receive from him without the minister noticing. However, to be able to absorb such an anointing upon a chosen vessel, one should make sure that the power is first on them. It is not only a matter of faith, but you have to make sure that there is a source of power in that vessel. Never try to build your faith on the Word by your mind, but let the Holy Spirit reveal the truth to you. Do not overemphasize the act of stepping out in faith when you know that there is no anointing on that particular minister. If there is no anointing on a particular minister, there is no point stepping out in faith to absorb any anointing from him because you will get nothing.

The *spill over anointing* is highly contagious such that it easily flows from you to people in your sphere of contact as they come into contact or interacts with you. What makes this type of anointing so unique is that it goes beyond church bars and doors and it operates even outside the church as it flows by association. For example, it spills over from teachers to students, from a manager to subordinates at the office, from parents to children and from friends to friends through relationships. To substantiate my claim with reference to scriptural evidence, it is recorded in Numbers 11:16 that when Moses found that his work was strenuous, he told the Lord, *"Lord I cannot take this burden* anymore." And the Lord said to Moses; *"Gather to Me seventy men of the elders of Israel, whom you know to be the elders of the people and officers over them; bring them to the tabernacle of meeting, that they may stand there with you. God took some of the anointing on his life and He put it on the seventy people. When the same anointing came on them, they started prophesying. The Spirit also came upon some people at home as their names were on the roll.* This is the character of manifestation of the *spill over anointing.*

These seventy received a portion of the *spill over anointing* upon them and began to function in judging the people.. You never read about them again except that what they did was to judge the people of Israel. Apparently they didn't become prophets neither were they priests but they became effective because they received the *spill over anointing* from Moses.

When Jesus sent out the one hundred and twenty, the anointing upon Him was transferred upon them, hence they operated in the same dimension of the anointing that Jesus functioned. This is the operation of the *spill over anointing*. It is further recorded in 1 Samuel 19:24 that Saul was told by Samuel to go and meet the prophets and the minute he joined them, the anointing upon the prophets spilled over upon Saul such that even though he had never prophesied before, he started prophesying too. This is because the anointing had spilled over from the prophets to him due to contagious association.

Practical Demonstration

During a ministerial session in one of our meetings, as I ministered the word, I was prompted by the anointing to call one of the sisters who had been listening attentively to the teaching of the word to come to the front. Unknowingly, she had been so much absorbing the anointing on me. I then called one of the young men who had an asthma attack to come and join her on the stage and then commanded the young lady to lay hands on the young man. Apparently, the sister had been sitting in front throughout the service and unknown to her; she had been absorbing the anointing that was flowing through me. As she laid her hands on the young man, she transferred the anointing and the young man fell under the power and asthma left him instantly and when he woke up, he was perfectly healed, Glory to God. This is the effect of the *spill over anointing*.

To reinforce an in-depth understanding of the operations of the *spill over anointing*, while in the same meeting, I randomly called out seven people who had been absorbing the flow of the anointing in the congregation to come forward and also called another group of seven people who were afflicted by various sicknesses to come and receive their healing. I then commanded the first group to lay hands on the sick at the same time, with each person laying hands on a person of his choice. As they simultaneously lay hands, all the sick people fell under the power and as they rose from the floor, every affliction had left them instantly. In other words, various sicknesses such as diabetes, TB, cancer and even HIV/AIDs had left them permanently.

On a separate occasion, I called one of the sisters in the congregation who had a lump of cancer on her breast. I then asked her to read a portion in one of my books entitled *"The Realm of Power To Raise The Dead"*. As she read that portion, she instantly absorbed so much anointing from the pages of the book such that while she was halfway through, she fell under the power and when she rose up from the ground, the lump on her breast had disappeared. This is how *the spill over anointing* operates. However, it must be expressly understood that this kind of anointing does not only flow from human vessels but can also flow from any other object that has retained the

19

anointing. For example, the minister's clothes, handkerchief, Bible or any other inanimate object.

3. Power Shot Anointing

This anointing is the most powerful substance in the realm of God's power. When it is administered upon a person, it is like receiving a cannonball in the stomach and one will be flung behind for several feet. It comes like a wave of power. It is called power shot anointing because of the gravity and intensity of power displayed during its flow or manifestation. This anointing comes with much power and force such that at times one can fall vehemently on the floor as if he had been hit by a hand of a man or shot by a machine gun. Although it lasts only for a moment, *power shot anointing* is very useful for blasting away very deep-rooted strongholds or strong demonic presence in an instant. What would have taken several praying sessions before a person experiences complete deliverance can be done in an instant with this *power shot anointing*.

The scriptural basis of this type of anointing is recorded in Mark 9:1427 whereby after the disciples of Jesus failed to cast out a demon from a boy, when the boy was brought to Jesus, he cast it out with so much power that it knocked the boy onto the ground before departing. In other words, Jesus demonstrated this type of anointing. Moreover, it is recorded in Acts 16:16 that when Paul and Silas were in Antioch, a girl who was possessed with a spirit of divination kept following them and disturbing them. Paul was provoked and he tapped into the realm of the power shot anointing such that he turned back and cast out the spirit and it departed instantly.

Besides deliverance, this type of anointing can also be administered when the minister wants the congregation to receive a heavy impartation of power especially when spiritual gifts are imparted and activated. Power is not only released or demonstrated when casting out demons. Instead, activation of spiritual gifts and releasing believers for the work of ministry also takes place under a heavy impartation of the anointing and in some cases it requires that the minister waves his hand towards the congregation with power so as to release that heavy dose of the anointing. It is called *power shot anointing* because it is released with power and because of the gravity, intensity and magnitude of power that is released upon the masses.

Practical demonstration

In a ministerial context, I told the congregation to be expectant and to open up their spirits because I wanted to impart the gifts of the spirit. I then shouted "*Are you ready for the dose of the anointing?*" By so doing, I wanted to raise a high level of expectancy so that their spirits are rightly positioned to receive the power of God. I then waved my hands with power towards the congregation and so much anointing was released into the atmosphere that got multitudes of people vehemently flying backwards and falling under the power and in the process, scattering chairs all over the place. That wave of power was so strong such that the people were break pedalled backwards before landing on the floor where they lay for quite some time of the floor before they regained their consciousness. This is how the power shot anointing is released.

During a different ministerial session, I called a young man who was for a long time possessed by a familiar spirit which made him very stubborn and violent. I then told him to be ready for the anointing that will set him free and carry him for years. He then stood in the middle of the aisle about twenty feet away from me. I then pointed my finger at him and shouted "*power*" and a sword of power went through him and the young man let out a scream and was flung several feet down the aisle before falling under the power. When he rose from the floor and gained his consciousness, he discovered that the demon had left him, glory to God!

4. ACCUMULATIVE ANOINTING OR BUILD UP ANOINTING

This is an anointing that builds up and creates its own spiritual atmosphere and climate as it is released in a particular place. This type of anointing starts as small as a cloud and as more is poured out from the Holy Ghost, it gradually accumulates and starts building up. It builds up in a similar manner as cumulative clouds of rain. It manifests itself like a *glory cloud*. The Bible occurs in Ecclesiastes that *if clouds be full of rain, they empty themselves on earth*. This is symbolic of how this anointing is formed because it is given birth to in the spirit as a result of a build-up of clouds of glory. Its nature of formation and character of manifestation is similar to the size of a man's hand which Elijah observed as he was praying for rain to fall after three and half years of drought. Although it starts as small as a man's hand, it can build up into clouds of rain up to a level where everyone in the congregation is slain in the spirit.

In other words, Elijah tapped into the realm of *accumulative anointing* and the more he prayed, the more the clouds of power accumulated until they reached saturation point and finally released abundant rain. Unlike other types of the anointing, the accumulative anointing does not come swiftly, speedily or instantaneously like a running tap of water, instead, it twinkles and builds up gradually until it fills the whole auditorium. A person who is not sensitive to the anointing or impatient might give up quickly thinking that the anointing is not moving through the congregation, yet in actual fact it's still building up. Sooner or later it will get everybody drowning in the anointing. Although its start slowly or gradually as it reaches its saturation point, it is so heavy and thick that whoever comes into contact with it falls under the power and stays on the floor for a while before recovering. The only challenge pertaining to the operation of the accumulative anointing is that it needs to be channelled in a specific direction in the same way cumulative clouds are channelled through a *cloud seeding*. Depending on the operation of the Holy Spirit, the nature of the work to be accomplished in the realm of the spirit, and of course the level or dimension of anointing the minister is operating, at times the build-up process of the anointing begins the instant a minister starts teaching the word, while in some cases it starts at the end of the preaching, hence the minister must always be sensitive to the build-up of the anointing.

However, what makes it distinct from other manifestations of the anointing is because it has a longer life span. It is not easily lifted up and it doesn't wean quickly. Instead, it stay much longer on the vessels as compared to other types of anointing. This type of anointing is powerful because as the anointing builds up gradually and progressively, there is a corresponding level of faith which also builds up in the congregation and by the time it stars flowing uncontrollably, the level of faith would have heightened so much that people are ready to receive. At times it takes quite some time for the faith level of some people to build up, hence this type of anointing creates a time for that build up process. Because of the considerable amount of time it takes for it to build up until it flows through the congregation, it gives a chance for spectators, doubters and those whose conductivity levels are low to also receive from God. This is because other types of anointings manifests so fast such that poor conductors of the anointing do not receive much but the accumulative anointing makes it easy for everybody to be touched by God. In the natural realm, clouds which takes time to build up in the atmosphere usually releases heavy rain than those which releases rain instantly. By the same token, the accumulative anointing produces a heavy rain of power which allows the power of God to infiltrate, permeate and sink deep into the people's bodies and spirits thereby dealing effectively with deep seated emotional, mental issues and strongholds which would not have been possible to deal with under the normal operation of the anointing. This is the main reason why the Holy Ghost releases the accumulative anointing in a meeting.

Practical demonstration

During a ministerial session, I sensed a build-up of an *accumulative anointing,* evidenced by a sudden change in the spiritual atmosphere. I then commanded that there was a cloud of anointing that was building up like a *glory cloud* in a certain section at the back of the congregation and as I released that cloud, it emptied so much power upon the congregation at the back such that everyone in that section fell under the power and instantly sicknesses and demons departed from them. It was as if a bucket of water has been splashed from a full tank upon the masses as they uncontrollably basked under the cloud of God's presence.

In a different meeting, I sensed a cloud of anointing build up at the centre of the alter and quickly called those who were heavily laden to come and jump into the pool of the anointing. As they came, the anointing kept building up until everybody was slain in the spirit. It started with one person falling under the power but the more they flocked into the alter, the more the received the touch of the anointing. That anointing was so heavy such that people lay on the floor for several hours before they could regain their consciousness and as they rose from the ground, there were numerous reports of healings and deliverance from sicknesses, mental disorders and emotional problems which had inflicted people for years.

5. BREATHING ANOINTING

This type of anointing works, operates and is released through breath. In other words, it is released by a vessel through breath and it travels through the waves of the air before it can manifests upon its intended recipients. It must be understood that the anointing has the exact properties similar to those of a wind. Once it has been released in a particular area, it moves through the waves of the air and it lingers in that environment or atmosphere for some time before it fades away. Depending on the gravity of its manifestation, in some cases, it can linger in the air for days. Paul gives a picture of the operation of this anointing when he says *a man born again is like wind which blows whenever he wishes, no one noes where it comes and where it goes.* This is how the *breathing anointing* operates.

23

The breathing anointing originated with God breathing His Spirit into Adam and Adam becomes a living being (Genesis 2:7). In other words, God breathed into Adam's nostrils and he received the anointing. This implies that the breath of God is *the anointing*. Moreover, to give you a historical background and insight into the phenomenon of the *anointing*, when God created man in the Garden of Eden in His own image and likeness, God gave man His own characteristics, traits and abilities. In other words, man was enabled by God to move in both the realm of the spirit to commune with God and also function in the realm of the natural and interact with animals. This means that when we are anointed, we have the same characteristics and abilities as that of God. Therefore, the anointing in simple terms can be referred to as an enablement from God to man while at the same time, man also inherits the qualities or the ability to impart the anointing that he has to others in his sphere of contact. In other words, the anointing represents the characteristics, traits and abilities of God himself. It is for this reason that the anointing is such a delicate and precious heavenly commodity, hence we should be interested in getting more of God's anointing to become more like Him by being transformed into His image and likeness. The good news is that God's anointing is available to every one of us and those who diligently seek it and are willing to use it for the extension of God's kingdom are the first candidates to be considered as recipients of this amazing divine treasure.

It is also recorded in John 20:22 that Jesus breathed His breath upon His disciples and said *"receive yee the Holy Ghost"* and as the Holy Ghost came upon them, He rubbed the anointing on them and they received the *anointing*. This implies that His breath travelled through the air and was imparted upon the disciples. Hence, in the realm of the anointing, there is such a thing called a *breathing anointing*. So, when there is a mighty move of the anointing in a particular place, it's because Jesus would have breathed His breath upon the congregation. Just like air which builds up in certain territories than in others, there are times when there is a buildup of the anointing as a higher concentration of the anointing than in other places. This is the most effective anointing because once it is administered upon a human vessel, it permeates his being, flows from the crown of his head to the soles of his feet, perambulating through every fibre of his being, every cell of his blood, it sinks deep even into the very bones and saturates one to the maximum spiritual capacity. In the process, it drives out demons, burns out blockages in the soul and heals every manner of sickness in the body.

Practical demonstration

In a ministerial context, I demonstrated the breathing anointing by taking a mike and breathed into it and multitudes in the congregation fell under the power as the breath of the Holy Ghost was released through the waves of the air and landed upon the masses. I demonstrate this type of the anointing a lot especially when I am ministering the healing anointing. As people stand in a queue awaiting their healings, I usually breathe upon their faces one by one and they fall under the power and as they wake up, they are instantly healed. In some cases as I blow towards the congregation, some people instantly receive miracle money in their wallets or notifications in their cell phones that money has been deposited into their accounts, others receive gold dust, diamonds and other precious stones as well as angel feathers. This is to show how powerful the breathing anointing is because you can breathe out anything you want to see manifested in the natural and since your spirit is loaded with Heavenly riches, as you breathe over the congregation, that wealth flows out from your spirit and is manifested through Miracle money and other divergent ways. The bottom line is that your spirit can breathe out anything be it healing, money, power, property and so forth because we are custodians of God's glory on earth as Christ dwells in our spirit.

During another ministerial session, I practically demonstrated the breathing anointing by breathing the Spirit of joy into the air. I then called out some people to come forward and breathe or inhale the breath in the atmosphere where I had released my breath. When they breathe in, they burst out laughing. I then commanded that the more you breathe in, the more Spirit of joy you will get and as they breathed in even more, they burst out laughing hysterically. I then blew towards the congregation and everyone in the congregation also laughed. In other words, they received an impartation of the *breathing anointing*.

6. OVERTAKING ANOINTING

The Bible presents a very striking, thrilling and remarkable divine experience about the overtaking anointing. It says in Amos 9:13 that *the plough man shall overtake the reaper.* As I meditated on this revelation, the Lord showed me recently in a divine encounter how time is running out and eternity is rushing in. In this experience of glory, I began to understand how, in the Book of Amos, the ploughman could overtake the reaper. In other words, the eternal realm was literally overtaking time in the natural and these are the very sacred, special and delicate moments into which we have been ushered in the calendar of God. Spiritually speaking, seeds of destiny are ready for reaping. In accordance with God's times and seasons, we are in a critical time of acceleration. We have stepped into (Amos 9:13), where *the ploughman shall overtake the reaper*. In other words, all of eternity is pouring into the present causing acceleration in the realm of the natural. Seeds that have been sown in the past, seeds of destiny, both good and evil, are full-grown and ready for reaping. As the realm of eternity is meshed with the present, we are witnessing a culmination of events as loose ends are being tied up before the return of Christ.

The realm of the *overtaking anointing* is the realm of speed and acceleration. In that realm of glory, things that would normally take ten years to happen will only take ten months and what could have taken the whole year to figure out will materialise in few seconds. There is a rapid maturity taking place in the body of Christ as the cloud of His anointing descends and blankets us corporately. Therefore, in this season, the Lord shall propel you into the future, catapult you to the higher realms of His presence. This is the essence of the overtaking anointing. The overtaking anointing is the one that while you are still preaching, people are already delivered by the anointing, while you are still waiting for your money to generate interest in the bank, you are already reaping a profit. It is a realm of acceleration. It doesn't allow you to wait long in order to see results of your seed, but while you are sowing, you are also reaping at the same time. This is because when we operate under the overtaking anointing we are instantly catapulted into the timeless dimension of eternity. In that realm, time does not exist hence we do not need to wait for us to receive things. As we release, we receive and as we speak, things manifest instantly.

In that realm, you don't have to wait for ten years to become a millionaire. Instead, as you release the anointing, you receive an instant message that a million rand has been deposited into your account. You don't have to wait for you to finish studying so that you can get a job, while you are studying, a job comes your way. The realm of overtaking anointing manipulates and alters time. When Elijah declared that *by this time tomorrow, a jar of four shall be sold for a shekel* (2 Kings 2-8:29), he was catapulted into the realm of *overtaking anointing*. And in that realm, as you speak it, your words travel swiftly in the spirit to cause all forces of divinity to work speedily to give birth to what you would have decreed in the spirit realm. That is why there is no waiting period. Unfortunately, many folks tend to preach and talk a lot about people waiting before receiving things from God and they quote how David waited in the caves before he became the King, because they have not yet caught the revelation of the *overtaking anointing*. Procrastination is not of God, especially in this end time season into which we have been ushered because God declared that *it shall come to pass that while they are still asking, I will answer*. This is the realm of overtaking anointing. Where then is waiting? It doesn't have a place in God at all. You don't have to join a company and wait for the next 10 years for your manager to die so that you can get promotion. Instead, with your first year of employment, you can be catapulted into the reality of overtaking anointing and be a manager. In your first year at university, you can be catapulted into the realm of overtaking anointing and be the SRC President; in your first year of doing business, you can tap into the realm of overtaking anointing and become a millionaire, glory to God!

In a practical sense, the *overtaking anointing* is the one that when you intend to release on one person, it ends up touching the whole congregation. In other words, it overtakes them. You impart it on one person and as he falls under the power and comes into contact with others, they too catch the same anointing. It is highly contagious. It is like a fame of fire which you ignite on one tree but then spreads to consume the whole forest. It operates by the law of association. Saul was not a prophet but when he joined a group of prophets, he was overtaken by the prophetic anointing and he started prophesying heavily with them. The *overtaking anointing* catapults one to high realms of glory, propels him to his destiny and causes him to see things that could have taken him years to figure out. It takes one to higher places and realms and deeper territories that he has never been.

Elijah also tapped into the realm of *overtaking anointing* at outran Ahab who rode of the best horse in the country. In other words, Elijah was carried or overtaken by the tidal wave of the spirit and ran with the speed of lightning, faster than King Ahab. The *overtaking anointing* enables us to accomplish the work of God with divine speed and a sense of urgency. It breakthrough and overtakes or touches even those who are resistant or not much yielded or not prepared to receive the anointing. When it flows over the congregation, it submerges anything that stands on its way, whether it's ready, prepared or not. *It is like a breakthrough anointing*

The greater truth is that Adam was born in a life of glory and he never had to wait for the earth to produce fruits. By virtue of the life of glory, Adam was exempted from going through the normal stages of plant conception, growth and maturity and just by sowing a seed; he was instantaneously catapulted right into the season of harvesting. This implies that plants and trees grew as each seed hit the ground. In other words, Adam did not have to wait to gather the harvest because waiting implies a space in time but the glory is eternity where everything is in the now. In the dimension of glory, the law of faith had broken the law of time hence everything produced fruits instantaneously. With God's glory, everything in the natural accelerates and manifest at a higher speed as is the case in the supernatural. In other words, the glory brings the supernatural and natural realms into harmony and function together for our good.

The Bible records in Amos 9:13, that, *"Behold the days are coming says the Lord, when the ploughman shall overtake the reaper and the treader of grapes him who sows seed".* This speaks of the season of the *overtaking anointing* into which we have been ushered in this end time dispensation. Prophetically speaking, by reason of the overtaking anointing, we have been accelerated into the realm of the supernatural, propelled by the law of faith in antagonistic to the limitations of time and catapulted into higher realms of glory. We are therefore living in a season and operating in a dimension whereby immediately after we sow a seed we see a harvest. In other words planting and harvesting are taking place concurrently or at the same time. Where then is the law of waiting? In a practical sense, our debts can be cancelled instantaneously and God is ready to release millions of wealth, property, mansions, houses, cars, private jets or business opportunities in a split of a second by reason of the *overtaking anointing.*

Moreover, in the life of glory and prosperity in the Garden of Eden, man did not even have to sow a seed in order to reap a harvest as is the case today. In the dimension of glory, the earth was completely fertile, fruitful and productive. Its times and seasons were different from what the situation is today. As a matter of fact, its order was harvesting first then seed time later. But after the fall, man got disconnected from the glory of God as God inhaled back His glory from Adam's body and at that moment man exited the dimension of glory and started experiencing drastic changes. That is why the bible records in Romans 3:23 that *for all have sinned and fallen short of the glory of God.* One of the changes which Adam experienced was in the order of sowing and harvesting. For example, the process of provision was no longer harvesting first and seed time later as it was in the beginning. Instead, the order was changed such that now seed time comes first then harvesting later, of which it takes time to wait for the harvest after sowing. That is why it is recorded in Genesis 8:22 that, *"while the earth remains, seed time and harvest, cold and heat, winter and summer and day and night shall not cease".* This came as a result of the curse. The current set up of things is that in order to harvest, one has to sow first and without a seed there is no harvesting but it was not like this during the former days of prime glory. Immediately after the fall, God demanded that man gives something and that is why Abel and Cain were instructed to give a sacrifice of which before the fall God never demanded Adam to give him anything. Even now God demands that one must not come into His presence empty handed (Deuteronomy 16:16). In other words, in order to receive something from God, you must give something and this could be in any form, for example time, effort, money or any

28

material possession. This is the essence of the law of sowing and reaping, planting and harvesting, giving and receiving.

Practical demonstration

In one of our meetings, I randomly called out a group of seven people from the congregation and told them to line up at the front and join hands to receive the anointing. I then touched the last person in the queue and imparted the anointing. Suddenly, it broke through and touched all of then causing them to fall under the power. As these seven fell and came into contact with those who sat in the congregation, suddenly, they too fell under the power and within few seconds that anointing had flowed to touch everybody in the auditorium.

In a second session, I took a bag and transferred the anointing upon it. I then threw it on a lady who was sitting at the front. As the bag came into contact with her, she went under the power and the anointing broke loose and flowed like a wave causing everyone in the congregation to fall under the power. In a different meeting, I released the overtaking anointing upon the congregation and declared that by the same time on the following day, all those who are seeking employment will be employed and miraculously on the exact time on the following day, we received reports of multitudes of people who had reported at the work place. In other words, the instant the anointing was released; there was a supernatural influence that caused all forces of divinity to move swiftly on behalf of everybody who needed a job, hence there was an instant manifestation in the natural realm. They did not have to wait for the natural processes of application and interviews but were catapulted straight into the level of working without undergoing all these formal stages of employment seeking.

I know of a man of God who prayed for a lady who needed a child and as the *overtaking anointing* was released upon her, she instantly fell pregnant and gave birth to a healthy child within three days. In other words, eternity had overtaken time in the natural, hence the lady needed not to wait for nine months to deliver the child. Although it boggles the mind and ruffles the feathers of those comfortable with the status quo, this is how we operate under the *overtaking anointing*.

7. BREAKTHROUGH ANOINTING OR CROSS OVER ANOINTING

This is an anointing of a breaker invested upon a vessel to bring about open doors and opportunities, breakthrough and open heavens over people's lives. A breakthrough is a divine intervention that comes when you have tried everything, toiled and tossed but just can't find a way. This is usually because there is something standing between you and your destiny that needs to be broken. For example between Egypt and Canaan there was a wall of Jericho and the Red sea, between Daniel and the end time revelation was the prince of Persia. There is ample scriptural evidence that unveils the divine truth that the reason why the children of Israel crossed over into Canaan and subdued many kingdoms was not necessarily because they had a well-trained army. Instead, it was because of the *breakthrough anointing* that their leaders had received from Moses through impartation (Numbers 11:25). The breakthrough anointing is what enables you to cross over, go beyond any limitations, obstacles or hindrances both in the natural and spirit realm.

There are three essentials needed for a break through to take place No 1. There must be a *breaker (An anointed vessel of God to action the process and bring about the breakthrough)* No 2. There must be an *object to be broken (a curse, a cage, a wall of resistance, demonic stronghold, poverty etc.)* No 3. A *beneficiary or recipient* of a breakthrough *(a person to receive or go through a breakthrough)*. During the breakthrough process, the anointing is released to break the walls of resistance and barriers. This is because the nature of the anointing is such that it is highly acidic, it dissolves and melts down every demonic walls and turns them it into liquid. It liquidates every demonic material used to stop you. When the Bible says *It shall come to pass that on that day, the burden shall be uplifted off your neck and the yoke be destroyed* because of the anointing, *it* speaks of the *breakthrough anointing.* Note that the phrase *"because of the anointing"* implies that the yoke can only be broken by the anointing and nothing else. This means that in the absence of anointing there is no breakthrough.

In most cases when Christians read about the fall of the walls of Jericho, they don't really get to catch a revelation of what exactly caused the walls to fall. Some people think that it was angels which demolished the walls of Jericho. Others think that it was the sound of the shouting which led to their collapse. It must be understood that the walls did not fall because of the shouting but because of the anointing encapsulated in that shouting. In other words, in the invisible realm, a breakthrough anointing was released through shouting or noise into the atmosphere that causes forces of divinity to release a corresponding power to crash down the walls. The power was not in the *shouting* but in the *anointing*. Shouting was a means of channelling the anointing. It is that anointing which was released into the atmosphere which changed the spiritual climate such that the walls melted and dissolved because of the anointing hence they came down. This is the same anointing which broke loose the chains of Saul and Barnabas when they were in prison in Acts. It is their worship and praises that released an anointing that shook the foundation of the prison and broke loose their handcuffs. It is not the loudness of their voices which brought about the breakthrough but the anointing encapsulated in their voices. For example, in a ministerial context, you can shout as loud as you want but if you are not anointed, you will accomplish little in the spirit realm. It is the anointing that is released through the shouting that makes a difference in the spirit.

It is a typical scenario in the body of Christ to find some Christians who are still struggling in their lives, in their finances or health because their ways are blocked by demonic powers. It is important in this case that a breakthrough anointing be released to set the captives free. In other words, the best medicine that deals with demonic strongholds is the breakthrough anointing. In actual fact, when Isaiah proclaimed *that it shall come to pass that on that day the burden shall be uplifted and the yoke destroyed because of the anointing,* he spoke about the breakthrough anointing. In the context of this scripture, the phrase *"yoke"* refers to a demonic bondage and he phrase *"that day"* speaks of this end time dispensation where the breakthrough anointing shall be released in increased measure to dismantle the powers of Satan. It is the anointing that uproots, dismantles and destroys all the powers of evil. In other words, it crushes, overthrows and completely destroys the trace of demonic powers. In cases where people are bound by witchcraft, generational curses, Satanism and magic, the *breakthrough anointing* is the key solution.

Practical demonstration

A certain man, seemingly vexed by life circumstances came to me and cried, *"I need a breakthrough in my prayer life. It does matter what I do. It's like there is a brick wall in front of me. Whatever I touch does not materialise. I have done everything that I know best but I seem not to be getting a breakthrough".* I then explained, "There are several reasons why a lot of people cannot receive a breakthrough from God. Firstly, there is unrepentance in the person's life. If sin is present, God will back away from you. God never fails. He always blesses. Only sin prevents His blessings. Sin gives the devil a legal foothold to steal, twist and manipulate your blessings. Secondly, there is resistance in your soul and will to the workings of God. Thirdly, there are certain blockages present in your life that are caused by powerful strongholds. Fourthly,

31

there are external blockages coming from people in your sphere of contact. Either the strongholds of those nearest and dearest to you or your own strongholds can stir the demonic presence in anyone of you to cause you problems. Fifthly, wrong concepts that are implanted in your souls. You have to bypass the barrier to the soul to get to the spirit. The enemy put on a spiritual shield in your mind to doubt and question the genuine move of God."

I then led the man in a prayer of repentance after which I summoned the demon causing this problem in this man to manifest. I stripped the legal rights of the demon and consigned it to the place of wrath. I then proceeded to explain to the man that the enemy has documents against him. In Jesus' office in heaven, He receives many petitions from the devil against His people for their wrongdoing. When Jesus told Peter that Satan demanded for him, it was not idle talk. The Lord said, *"Simon, Simon! Indeed, Satan has asked for you, that he may sift you as wheat.* (Luke 22: 31) Satan had legal grounds to petition Jesus for the right to sift Peter like wheat because he denied the Lord three times. In your records, your ancestors worshipped gods. Jesus had to contract with the enemy at a very high level and purchase you with His blood. When your ancestors worshipped these gods, it opened the door for the enemy to take possession of your family tree. You came under the shield of gods. This is why the power of God could not penetrate into your spirit. Furthermore, you were not totally committed to God. Jesus is a God of rules. He too has to observe rules. There is only one way for Jesus to help, and that is the way of grace. When you prayed the prayer for grace, God could then give you grace and deliver you.

8. TRANSITIONAL ANOINTING

The transitional anointing is a type of anointing that is manifested whenever God wants to bring about a change in the seasons of the spirit. In other words it comes with a change in seasons of God. A *transitional anointing* is therefore that anointing that is able to bring forth a clear cut change or transformation. For example, if there are new things that God wants to usher into the church, they can be easily be brought into manifestation by way of a *transition anointing*. To cement this revelation with reference to scriptural evidence, David was anointed three times and every time he received the anointing, he moved from one level of power to the next. This is described by the nature and manner in which it flows or operates. It is an evolutional anointing. It brings about sudden changes and turnarounds in situations and circumstances. It has an ability to change an atmosphere and spiritual climate of a place. It establishes a long lasting effect or impact upon recipients. Its presence makes the atmosphere so heavy, so thick and pregnant with the power of God. When it moves, at times you can literally see mist or raindrops falling. At times it can bring about a cool breeze or tangible results. It is refreshing and uplifting in nature. As it comes upon man, it catapults them to their level of calling.

Whenever God needed to move a particular generation from one transition to another, He need the three offices to function to the fullness, whether through one man or through three different men for the three different offices. Moses lived in an important transition. There are transitions in our lives; there are transitions in a family; there are transitions in a generation. The world today is going through a transition economically. Transition period is very critical since if it is not bent the right way the deformity will continue for the rest of years to come. So, in the transition period God has to see to it that all three offices must function. All three offices have to function whether through one person who stands in all three or in three separate persons who stand in one each. He needed that for the perfection of that generation in the Old Testament. Samuel stood between the period of the judges and the period of the kings. He was the marker pen in between. On one side were the judges; on the other side were the kings. He was the key guy who saw the transition. Therefore, God needed the three offices to function fully during this period of transition. Samuel functioned in all three offices to the fullness. If God could find three people to put the various anointing, He would have used all three.

The Bible says when Samuel was born, there was no open vision. There was no revival. He was born into a dead, dried and decayed generation. The Bible even said in the book of (I Samuel 2) there was no open vision. In other words, there was no prophetic ministry and no prophetic voice. What about the priests? They would help themselves to the food while it was sacrificed. They were so caught up in the death of sin such that they were eating the meat meant for sacrifices. They had a form of religion without the power. There was no anointing. They were not anointed. They were supposed to be but they were not. What about the judges? Unheard of, everyone did what was right in their own eyes. They had no leader. Practically God had no office that functioned at all, not because He did not want to but because there was no vessel. God finally found Samuel and started training Samuel to hear His voice. Before that, Samuel was waiting on God. He was serving in the temple faithfully. In spite of all the things he saw around him, he was faithful. If ever you live in a dead generation, one key is to be faithful and you will be the very key to the revival there. The three types of anointing of God came on his life to stand in all three offices. God

33

began to use Samuel as a transition from the old wicked generation to the new one.

In a practical sense, the Body of Christ is currently going through transition as the transitional anointing is released in greater measure. The following are areas where transition is taking place. Firstly, there is a transition from operating in the realm of the anointing into the realm of glory. In other words, as believers mature in the realm of the anointing, they are going to be catapulted into a higher realm of power which is the realm of glory. Secondly, there is a transition from the realm of ordinary miracles into creative miracles of glory. While over decades the body of Christ have witnessed miracles such as cripples walk, blind eyes opened, and the sick healed, the miracles which God is releasing in this season are so deep such that they even believers themselves shall be shocked. For example, there shall be more mass resurrections of people from the dead around the world. Thirdly there is a transition from the old into new waves of manifestation whereby miracle money, supernatural debt cancellation, supernatural oil, gold dust and silver stones and other precious stones are increasingly taking centre stage in the realm of the miraculous as God is unveiling new waves of His glory. Therefore, in this end time season, believers are yet to witness brand new manifestations from heaven, things which they have never seen or heard of. God is not able to use some people mightily and unleash His creativity because many are still holding on to the old wine skins, hence God cannot go beyond the level of revelation which a man fathoms. Old manifestations such as people falling under the power, laughing, shaking hysterically under the anointing shall give way to new manifestations such as translation, transportation in the spirit, increased visitation to the throne room, people floating under the power as God unveils His level of creativity.

Practical demonstration

In one of my meetings, I demonstrated to the congregation that there is a drastic transition taking place in the Body of Christ as God is introducing new spiritual manifestations and elevating believers to deeper realms of the Spirit. I told them that rather than God touching people to pay for their expenses or give them money, angels are going to deposit money directly into their accounts. I then released angels to deposit money into their accounts, wallets, pockets, and bags and then commanded the people to search in their wallets and bags and multitudes came forward with evidence of having received Miracle money. I also commanded the accompanying new manifestations such as gold dust, diamonds and angel feathers to appear and many received them either soaked in the palm of their hands, on their clothes and on the floor.

In another meeting I declared that a new wave of miracles, signs and wonders are increasingly being released in the Body of Christ as God is unveiling to us, the deepest and most sacred territories of the Glory Realm. I commanded creative miracles of glory upon the congregation and those with bald hair received hair, those with holes in their teeth received gold teeth, and new limbs and other body parts were created in places where previously they did not exist, glory to God!.

9. STATIONARY VERSUS FLOWING ANOINTING

A stationary anointing is an anointing that is lying dormant upon a vessel and has not yet been activated, stirred or provoked into manifestation. It is like the still waters in a well that have not yet been stirred into an overflow. It does have great potential to overflow powerfully. However, it has not yet been activated or awakened into manifestation. It must be expressly understood that it doesn't necessarily mean that every time the anointing is present, there will be violent manifestations. The Bible says when Jesus raised the only son of the widow of Nian in Luke 7:11-17 , *He touched the coffin and the bearers stood still.* In other words, by virtue of touching the coffin, the anointing was transferred or imparted into the dead body. However, that anointing was stationary. It only started operating the instant Jesus spoke and said, *"Young man I say to you arise"* and he arose from the dead. In other words, that anointing was activated by a spoken word into manifestation. It could be observed in the realm of the anointing that depending on the nature of manifestation of the Holy Spirit, sometimes the anointing does not flow and nothing will happen, even though the anointing is present on a vessel or on an object. When the Holy Spirit manifest Himself in the form of a river, the anointing will flow but if He manifests like a well, the anointing will not flow although it is present. This is a *stationary anointing.* It is present but not moving or manifesting. You not only have to be sensitive to the anointing but you also have to be sensitive whether the anointing is flowing or not. If the anointing is not flowing, you cannot do anything. You have to wait until the anointing begins to move, and then you act accordingly as the Holy Spirit directs you. Hence, there is such a thing as a *stationary anointing* and a *flowing anointing* in the same service.

Smith Wigglesworth tapped into these dimensions of the anointing hence he declared in one of his services *"If the Holy Ghost does move, I move the Holy*

35

Ghost". This means he had learnt how to provoke the stationary anointing of God to flow. At times the anointing is stationary because God wants us to tap into the realm of faith to provoke the anointing to move. Stationary anointing goes with the *general presence* while flowing anointing goes with the *manifest presence*. It is recorded that in the beginning of creation in Genesis 1:2, *the Holy Ghost was hovering over the earth*. In other words, He was stationary but the moment God spoke and said *let there be light*, the Holy Ghost began to move and went forth to birth those things which God spoke into manifestation. This is the case of *stationary versus flowing anointing*. The reason why Paul admonished the brethren *not to be quick to lay hands* is because he was conscious of the character of manifestation of the anointing, that at times it is stationary, hence rather than rushing into the act of laying hands, brethren should take an initial step to stir, activate and provoke the anointing into manifestation.

Practical Demonstration

During a service, I touched the pulpit and said, "*I have transmitted the anointing onto this pulpit but the anointing is not flowing. It is stationery.*" I then called a young man to come forward to touch the pulpit. Nothing happened. I then I touched the pulpit again and said, *the anointing is now flowing*. This anointing has the spirit of joy. The same young man went up and touched the pulpit and this time around, he started laughing hysterically in the Spirit. In the same meeting, I told the congregation that the anointing is present and has filled the whole spiritual atmosphere in the auditorium but its stationary. I then told them that the anointing is now moving and the instant I said it, there were manifestations all over the auditorium as people fell under the power, and started laughing and shaking hysterically. I then commanded again that the anointing was stationary and the instant I said it, the manifestations stopped and there was a complete silence. This is how the stationary and flowing anointing is demonstrated.

10. TRANSMITTABLE OR TRANSPORTABLE

ANOINTING

It is a divine truth that the anointing flows like electricity or water. It will flow from one person to another. Therefore, the anointing is not only a tangible substance and a heavenly materiality; instead, it is transmittable or transferable. *It can be transmitted from one person to another, or transferred from one through another.* Evidently, Jesus operated in the realm of transportable anointing when He called His twelve disciples to Him and gave them power against unclean spirits, to cast them out, and to heal all manner of sickness and all manner of disease (Matthew 10:1). In other words, there was an impartation of the anointing. The Word of God says in John 3:34 that Jesus had the Spirit without measure, so when He sent forth the Twelve, He gave them power. Where did He get this power? We saw in Acts 10:38 that *"God anointed Jesus of Nazareth with the Holy Ghost and power"*. That means that anointing flowed from God into Jesus and then from Jesus into His disciples. Often, even in ministry, something is transferred from one person to another. The Word of God says in the 34th chapter of Deuteronomy that Joshua had the same spirit of wisdom that Moses had, because Moses had laid his hands on him (Deuteronomy 34:9 9) and Joshua the son of Nun was full of the spirit of wisdom; for Moses had laid his hands upon him (Deuteronomy 34:9). Evidently some of that same spiritual wisdom and power Moses was anointed with was transferred to Joshua by the laying on of hands, for the power of God is transferable.

This is undeniably a very high level anointing. Through this anointing, one can enter into the realm of divine transportation in the spirit and pray for people thousands of miles away and God can touch them. There is no distance in the spirit. The anointing can be transmitted through satellite, television channels, radio frequency, books and these days, people can receive the power, anointing, deliverance and healing through television regardless of where they are in the world. As you are reading this book now, the transmittable anointing is coming upon you. The anointing originates from the Holy Ghost and moves by the frequency of the waves of the spirit through the air to its intended destination.

There is a lot that people can achieve under this anointing especially in this end time dispensation whereby the work of God has to be accomplished with a sense of urgency. This anointing can either allow the ministers to carry the power of God to distant places of the world or even transport the ministers themselves to various parts of the world to minister the gospel. Philip taped into this realm of anointing and *was carried by the tidal wings of the Spirit from Samaria to Azotus*. Elijah functioned a lot in this realm to the extent that he would disappear and appear at his own will. Elisha tapped into this realm when *his spirit followed Gehazi when he was fraudulently collecting goods back from Naman*. Paul tapped into this realm when he told the Corinthian church *that though he was absent in the body, he was with them in the spirit*. This is such a spectacular realm of the anointing. Philosophically speaking, it appears that this level of anointing is likely to replace the airline system because in this dispensation, many people will be transported to different parts of the world by the spirit to perform specific ministerial tasks.

Practical Demonstration

In one of our meetings, I demonstrated the transmutability of the anointing by asking about twenty one people to stand in a queue in front of the congregation. I then touched the first person on the queue and all of them fell under the power as the anointing was transferred from that person to the rest of them. In the same meeting, I told a sister at the back of the auditorium to get ready for the anointing. I said, *"I am going to touch this pulpit here in front, and the anointing is going to bounce onto the lady at the back."* I touched the pulpit, and the woman screamed and fell on the floor.

On another occasion, I prayed for a man who was insane and lived in another continent over the phone and commanded a demon of insanity to leave and he went under the power and the demon left and he came back to his normal senses. In this case, the anointing travelled or was transported through the waves of the air and located him in a twinkling of an eye and brought about the manifestation.

11. SPECIAL OR PECULIAR ANOINTING:

In the realm of God's power, there is such a thing called a *special anointing.* I'm convinced beyond a shadow of doubt that God is going to use some people in peculiar ways in these days, but they first must be sure that the peculiar unction or anointing is there. This is a kind of anointing that is peculiar, uncommon, and unusual to ordinary life. Its manifestation in the realm of God's power is such that it doesn't flow all the time but manifests whenever God does something special. It is a divine truth that every believer is anointed to *some* degree whenever the Spirit wills and to the level that they are willing to be used by Him. However, the Lord does grant special anointing to certain individuals who seem to be able to operate in a *higher* degree of various gifts.

The greater truth is that God will anoint you for whatever He has called you to do, but He anoints some people to minister in special ways, too. Some of us are anointed with *special anointings* and such anointings on ministries bring forth marvellous results. The Bible unveils the reality that there are special anointings in the gifts of the Spirit (1Corinthians:12:7-11. 1Corinthians12:28) and special anointing in the area of helps, administrations, and so forth (1Corinthians 12:28). These special anointings are granted by the *Lord* for whatever reason He chooses and they are not something that someone can just simply call upon at their *own* discretion. It is as the Spirit wills (1Corinthians 12:11). Such special anointing produces new operations and special manifestations that are unique, peculiar and uncommon to a generation. It is evident that the only time the word *"special"* is used in the New Testament is in relation to the special miracles that God wrought by the hands of the apostle Paul in Acts 19:11. What made these miracles *"special."*? To begin with, they were unique one time occurrences. From the Biblical record this was the only time something like this happened in the ministry of Paul, much like Peter's shadow in (Acts 5:15).

Kenneth Hagin in his encounter with the realm of special anointing says,

> *"Jesus told me to kneel down before Him. When I did, He laid His hand upon my head, saying that He had called me and given me a special anointing to minister to the sick.* (Kenneth Hagin, I Believe In Visions, p. 51). He laid His hand on my head and said, "I've called thee and have anointed thee and have given unto thee a special anointing to minister to the sick." He said,

> *"Tell the people exactly what I told you. That is, you tell them you saw me. Tell them I spoke to you. Tell them I laid the finger of my right hand in the palm of each one of your hands. Tell them the healing anointing is in your hands."*

Why? It's because he wants you to believe. It is evident across a broad spectrum of Christian faith in our generation that there are key and specific individuals who seem to operate in certain areas with a greater anointing than others. Again, this is something that the Lord anoints them to do for a specific reason and it is not something that we, on our own can just scoop up at will.

For Example, Smith Wigglesworth was given a special anointing and used by God in a special ministry of raising the dead. It is said that He would not allow anybody from his neighbourhood to die or depart from this earth without his permission. God used a man called William Brenham in a special way such that any germs or bacteria that came into contact with his body died instantly and even scientists evidenced it in his time. Bringing together different pieces of the brain after someone was crushed by a car into pieces is one of the special manifestations of supernatural power which God performed through this man. God can use you in a special way.

We can define and understand the special anointing by watching its manifested work upon the lives of those it comes upon. Bezaleel and Aholiab received special skill in metal works, jewellery and embroidery (Exodus 31: 1-6). The way you received the anointing will be peculiar to you in your situation. There may be similarities with others but the way the anointing comes on your life will be special and peculiar to you. Some people get warm when the anointing comes on their life. Some people feel their legs moving. Some people stand up a bit. Some people believe that when the anointing is there, your hair stands up. Remember we are dealing with what we call side effects of the manifestations. Therefore, do not take the side effects and build some theology upon these side effects. However, we need to touch on this subject so that we could have some understanding of the various forms of manifestation of the anointing. Now, the point that we are driving at is this, we must learn to recognize how the anointing manifests in our own life. We can thank God for how He manifests in others' lives. We must learn to recognize how He manifests in our life. If He manifests in your life through a warm sensation then that is peculiar to you. If He manifests through shaking, that is another individual peculiarity. The only thing that is strange is the peculiar manifestation of the anointing. There is such a thing as peculiar anointing. Some types of manifestation of anointing are very dignified. Some may not look so dignified.

I'm bringing this up because I believe some extraordinary things are going to happen before long. I believe we're going to see some things over in this area of anointing that we haven't seen before. I want to prepare you for them so you won't miss them or draw back from them simply because you haven't seen anything like them before. I want you to be ready to move with God.

Practical demonstration

In one of my meetings I made a public declaration that God has given me a special anointing for the multitudes across the globe. I then instructed the masses that I was going to demonstrate a glimpse of that anointing and told them that I'm not going to touch anybody but speak a word and when that happens, every sickness, challenge, disease or infirmity will disappear. I then stood in front of the congregation and the Spirit of the Lord began to move mightily upon the congregation to the extent that not even one person remained standing. As they rose from the ground, multitudes reported having been healed from HIV/AIDS, asthma, diabetes, cancer, delivered and received instant breakthroughs.

12. FRESH/ NEW ANOINTING OR SEASONAL ANOINTING

This is an anointing that flows when God is doing a new thing in a particular season. It must be understood that God moves in times and seasons and each time He moves, He brings forth new anointing as He unveils a new revelation of His being. Whenever we enter a new season, God releases fresh anointing for that particular season. The old manna gets to be replaced by the new one. A cool breeze is sent from the river that emanates from the Throne of God to the nations. When God says,

See, I'm doing a new thing, can't you perceive it as it springs forth? (Isaiah 43:19).

He is talking about the *new anointing,* new experiences, and new encounters in the realm of the spirit. They are new anointings in the sense that they have not been released before; they are fresh straight from the centre of God's throne. When the Bible says that we must repent before God so that times of refreshing may come from the presence of God, it actually speaks of the fresh anointing. There are times whereby some people get weary and exhausted in their Christian walk due to confrontation with tough situations and circumstances. However God releases a river of refreshing waters (*refreshing anointing*) from His presence so that the masses are refreshed, energised and strengthened to continue with the race they have started.

Moreover, the *new anointing* also comes with accepting of a new responsibility. When a Christian accepts a new responsibility, he should be anointed by the Holy Spirit for that task. When a pastor is called to a new church he should be anointed by the Holy Spirit. Any new task to which a child of God is chosen and any new responsibility that God has given to him is so important that the Holy Spirit should anoint him upon the assumption of his new responsibility. Whenever David was appointed a position, at each stage he was anointed. Likewise, as the Christian ministers and continues to fulfil the work to which God has called him, he should constantly be being filled with the Spirit. When God calls, He qualifies, He equips and He prepares. When a Christian is called to a new responsibility, he needs to be equipped. Hence, he needs to be anointed by the Holy Spirit as God appropriates to him what he needs to fulfil his new calling and equips him for that calling. This is a kind of anointing that you can release in a revival meeting to renew their vigour and energise them with the refreshing river of God's presence. As this new anointing is released in this end tome season, new mantles will fall upon the masses and shall give birth to new manifestations and operations of the Spirit such as the fall of the golden rain manifested through gold dust, silver stones, diamonds and the dew from Heaven.

Practical demonstration

In one of my meetings as I ministered, the place was extremely hot such that we had to literally keep all windows, doors and any other possible openings open. I then told the congregation that God is releasing a fresh and new anointing and as I took a step of faith to release it, all of a sudden a cool breeze filled the whole auditorium in the same way it filled the upper room at Pentecost. That presence was so refreshing, energising and rejuvenating such that no one wanted to leave that place and many were healed and delivered without anybody touching them. That was a release of a *fresh anointing*.

13. REFRESHING AND RESTORATION ANOINTING OR REVIVAL ANOINTING

This anointing comes to restore someone after he has lost something. The Bible says *repent so that the times of refreshing and restoration may come from the presence of the Lord.* This implies the *refreshing anointing* because it is the anointing that comes from the presence of God. This type of anointing usually comes through repentance. When you have been so worked out, discouraged, and drawn yourself away from the presence of God, you need a refreshing and restoration anointing so that you can make a fresh start.

You get to identify this anointing by the character of its manifestation. Usually when it comes upon the congregation, it will draw multitudes into deep worship and reverence where multitudes cry and weep for long before God. When that anointing is at work, incessant spiritual cries, prayers and worship are seen arising simultaneously from all sides of the congregation as the masses are uncontrollably basking under the reverence of the glory of God. Mixed sounds of laughter, exhilaration and weeping mingled with quiet music flowing from a sound system echoes through the congregation. Under such circumstances even the minister himself cannot do anything but join the flow. It is through these sacred moments that many are healed and delivered from deep seated emotional issues as they pour out their emotions before God.

14. THE RESURRECTION ANOINTING OR ANOINTING TO RAISE THE DEAD

This is a type of anointing that is used to raise the dead. In this end time dispensation, many people are going to tap into this type of anointing to display the power of God in a mighty way in the area of raising the dead. The most powerful, undisputable, unquestionable way to prove that Jesus was raised from the dead is to raise other people from the dead. When Jesus said *greater things than these shall we do* (John 14:12), one of those things which shall form the central theme of greater works especially in these end times is the raising of the dead. There is a large outcry in heaven for souls who are dying on a daily basis without salvation. The Bible says *there is great joy in heaven over one sinner who repents*(Luke 15:10). This implies that on the other side of the coin, there is great grief, sorrow, pain over the death of souls who depart without repentance. Therefore, God is releasing in greater measure a sacred and special type of anointing upon his servants by grace to accomplish certain tasks. The Bible says *If the same spirit that raised Jesus from the dead lives in us, then we are also empowered by the same spirit to raise the dead.*

Ezekiel's narrative in Ezekiel 37:1-14, of his experience with God in the valley of dry bones is not just a story as many believers have portrayed. Instead, it has a deep revelation encapsulated in it as gives a clear prophetic picture of how a resurrection is to be performed. The step by step process which God lead Ezekiel through is not just a story but a pictorial representation and portrait of how to raise the dead. According to Ezekiel, the breath of God blew over the valley of dry bones, and it became a mighty army. In the context of this revelation, the breath of the Almighty speaks of the *resurrection anointing*. In other words, the breath of God is what causes the dead to rise back to life. As a matter of fact, God showed to Ezekiel that a resurrection is not something which man does alone using his faith. Instead, it is a spiritual operation in which God partners with a man to give birth to a resurrection in the spirit realm. Our responsibility is therefore to speak God's word in faith and God's duty is to cause a supernatural manifestation. The reason why God asked Ezekiel "*Son of man can these bones live again?*" is not because God did not know, instead this was a rhetoric question meant to gauge Ezekiel's level of faith and revelation for a resurrection. In other words, God wanted to ascertain the level of revelation which Ezekiel had concerning a resurrection because God cannot use a man beyond the level of revelation he has. Therefore, this unveils the divine truth that *faith* and *revelation* are critical keys to the resurrection of the dead. Therefore in the same way God asked Ezekiel, *son of man can these bones live again?*, God is asking believers in this dispensation the same question; *can these dead be raised?*. This is because God requires that we reach out to him in faith in order to move in the realm of resurrection. In this end time season, God is raising a distinct breed of believers upon whom He is inculcating the grave to raise the dead, for His glory.

Practical Demonstration

In my own personal experience with God, I have had a window of opportunity to be mightily used by God in this sacred ministry as I was catapulted into the realm of God's omnipresence to pray for two people whom God raised back to life in mighty and power, a similar case to that of the resurrection of Jairus' daughter who was on the verge of death by the Lord Jesus Christ. The first resurrection encounter was that of a young lady who was on the verge of death for having failed to adhere to a medical prescription by overdosing tablets and during the early hours of the morning, it was brought to my attention by her grandmother that she would not see dawn. I then strategically used the lady as a point of contact and gave a prophetic instruction for her to lay her hand on the victim's stomach and as she did, I then released the *resurrection power* on her and instantly, the young lady was raised back to life. The other case was the resurrection of a young man who had suffered from a long illness and was on the verge of death as medical doctors had entirely given up on him but amazingly, God raised him back in power. Since then, my faith to raise the dead skyrocketed and it is my daily consciousness to seek for new avenues of power and opportunities to raise the dead for God's glory.

The reality of being awakened into the *realm of resurrection power* was like an experience of a man visiting a new planet for the first time. It was like waking up from a long slumber and delving into a pool of refreshing waters. A revelation was dropped into my spirit that you don't necessarily have to be present at the death scene in order to see the dead being raised. It's because this is a spiritual case that needs to be handled spiritually although physical presence might be necessary for the salvation of those who would have witnessed the resurrection. It was then that God revealed to me the divergent realms of resurrection encapsulated in this writing such as *the resurrection by omnipresence*. This is a scenario whereby a believer taps into God's omnipresence and uses another person as a point of divine contact to release the *resurrection power* upon a victim even when thousands of kilometres away. The other critical aspect which I was awakened into is the reality that contrary to what multitudes of people think, it is relatively easy to raise a person from the dead. It takes a childlike faith to believe and take God at His word as well as revelation, to be catapulted into that realm. That is why I strongly contend in this writing that,

It is easy to raise a man from the dead than it is to heal a religious Christian from a headache.

It takes just one step out of your comfort zone and convictions of ordinary life of wavering faith, unbelief and mediocrity, to raise the dead. However, if you still do not know who you are in Christ, in terms of your inheritance, legal rights and privileges as a believer, you will not able to step up to your position of son-ship and authority to partake of that which is legally and rightfully yours. But if you are fully inundated in the depths of God's presence and rightly positioned to go against the natural order of things, and you are not scared to take a risk of faith, then raising the dead shall be to you like a walk through a park.

While some ignorant believers might marvel at the idea of raising the dead, paradigms are shifting in this season as raising the dead and healing the sick shall come naturally to every believer. To partake of this abundant grace, you just need to infuse your spirit with God's word to the point that you become a walking demonstration of scripture. The resurrection power of God is resident in the extreme quarters of your spirit, hence you need to give the world something to talk about by showcasing this amazing treasure from within you. Remember that *you have treasures in earthen vessel* hence; the resurrection power of God is one of the hidden treasures that you have to unleash for within you to re-create your world. The other simple but integral principle you should take cognisance of is the *law of contagious association* because it matters most who you associate with when it comes to addressing pertinent cases of resurrection. The *resurrection anointing* is highly contagious, that is why if one person raises the dead in your church, city or sphere of contact, it becomes easy for others to catch the flame and be catapulted into the realm of raising the dead such that within a twinkling of an eye, the whole city will be moving in the realm of raising the dead and shaking the world. It is highly imperative in this regard not to use the previous generation but God's word as a yardstick or benchmark to measure your standard of performance because your sphere of contact can be a major obstacle, impediment or stumbling block to moving in the realm of resurrection. For example, if no one has ever raised someone from the dead in your sphere of contact or church, it doesn't necessarily mean that the dead cannot be raised. Instead, you can distinguish yourself as a pioneer of the *resurrection movement* and be the first in your community or city to break the *World Resurrection Record* through charting new frontiers, breaking fallow ground, demarcating boundaries and setting new trends in raising the dead as if you are waking up people from a slumber. There are also certain misconstrued Christian teachings that can deactivate or short-circuit God's ability in a man to raise the dead hence precaution must be taken concerning what you feed your spirit with, who you listen to or take instructions from in pursuit of such critical matters as raising the dead.

15. Double Portion Anointing

This is a mega anointing or double dose of the anointing released for a massive supernatural harvest. It is a magnified or multiplied anointing given to individuals to accomplish tasks to greater or unimaginable proportions as compared to others. The term *double portion* does not mean something multiplied by itself, instead the term Double portion implies a measure of anointing that has been greatly enlarged, multiplied, increased exorbitantly, superfluous, measureless or heightened. The double portion of the anointing is actually the mantle because a mantle is an anointing that has graduated or thickened as one advances in a particular office. The scriptural basis of this revelation is found in 2 Kings 2:9 whereby in his capacity as a successor, Elisha asked for—and received—a *"double portion"* of Elijah's anointing. That doesn't mean there are two Holy Spirits—there is just one. What Elisha called a *"double portion"* we could term a *"double measure"* of the anointing to stand in the same office. The thing that was special about this anointing was the added dimension. It's the same anointing, except a different measure. When Elisha asked Elijah for the *double portion* of His spirit, what he meant was that he wanted a double portion of that anointing of God to stand in the office of prophet. That is why it is recorded that he did twice as many miracles as Elijah.

It is a typical scenario in the body of Christ that not everyone has caught a revelation of what a *double portion* of the anointing is all about. As a result of this confusion, many are seen chasing after the anointing upon men of God with the aim of receiving a *double portion*. It must be understood that God anoints men and women to stand in specific offices and what determines whether you shall receive the *double portion* of the anointing is not how hard you have chased after the anointing but it's the type of office and calling upon your life. The truth is that a double measure of anointing would only be available from someone who is called in the same office as you are. Therefore, you will not be able to receive a double portion of a person who is called in an office that is different from yours because the notion of *double* implies an increase or build-up of the measure that you already have (*For example, if you're called to be a pastor, you don't need the prophet's anointing. Elisha was called to the office of prophet, however*). Elisha received a *double portion* of the anointing from Elijah because both of them were called in the same prophetic office, hence Elisha wanted to build up from the level of prophetic anointing which he already had, hence he moved in greater depths of power and the anointing more than ever before.

Moreover, the *double portion* anointing comes upon those who have been entrusted with greater responsibility in the kingdom. Every time one migrates from a local church vision to a national one, then regional, then continental, then global, a double portion of anointing is released to enable him to handle challenges at a higher level than before. Moreover, the *double portion* anointing rests upon those individuals who have stretched themselves to the limit of their spiritual capacity such that they are ready to mi-

46

grate to higher deeper and newer realms of the anointing. As you graduate through progressive levels of anointing by applying what you already have, more volumes of the anointing are increasingly released upon you. In other words, it is your capacity to receive that determines how much you shall receive.

Practical demonstration

I remember the time when I completed my Degree at university and now it was my time to leave the campus. Just because God had lifted me to operating in high levels of the anointing more than anybody else at campus, everyone was so excited about my departure because they were going to receive a *double portion* of the anointing upon my life since I was heading away to a faraway place. After explaining and airing the confusion relating to the notion of double portion, I eventually consented to having a meeting where I would make an impartation of the double measure of the anointing a requested. As I took a step of faith to release the anointing amongst a group of power hungry and zealous believers, declaring *"Receive the double portion"*, an unusual ball of anointing hit them, infiltrated deep into their spirits as they shook hysterically before they finally lay unceremoniously under the power. However, although there was a tangible evidence of everybody having received the anointing, the young man who had walked so closely with me in ministry is the one who received it. This was evidenced by the greater dimension of power which he manifested after my departure. Those who were just zealous to receive the anointing of course received a doze of the anointing, however since it was not something solid, they were never established in that anointing.

16. THE CORPORATE ANOINTING

This is the anointing that is collectively given to a group of people in a church or ministry by virtue of fellowship, association, partnership or membership. The whole church collectively has the anointing of all. When believers come together to worship and praise God, His glory can manifest in their midst. When the Bible talks about *How pleasant it is for brethren to dwell together in unity* (Psalms 133:1) and describes that *it is like oil poured on the head of Aaron and running down his beard*, in actual fact it speaks of the *corporate anointing* because it is released only when brethren are gathered to together in unity. It is for the reason of corporate anointing that Paul warned believers not to abandon the fellowship. This is because there are certain types of blessings or anointing which a believer can never receive by himself. Such blessings or anointing are released only when people are in a congregation. There are times when God releases an anointing corporately over the whole body of Christ especially when he wants to accomplish a specific purpose in a season. There are certain blessings that flow according to the grace of ministries hence a believer must be careful which ministry he belongs to. Usually the strength of the ministry or leader will determine how the corporate anointing flows.

17. THE COMMANDING, DIRECTIVE OR AUTHORITATIVE ANOINTING

This kind of anointing comes with a greater dimension of authority. It is commanding, authoritative and directive in nature. The Bible records an incident in Luke 7:8 whereby a centurion said to *Jesus' I am a man under authority, I say to this do this and he does and to that one go there and he goes*. The commanding anointing works in a like manner. It operates in such a way that if you command a person to do something under this anointing, he does exactly as you say. If you say to the person jump, he jumps under the anointing, if you say laugh, he laughs under the anointing and if you say sit, he sits under the anointing; if you command him to run, he does exactly as you say. Jesus tapped into this realm of anointing when He was choose His disciplines. He said to Peter, *"follow me"* and without any resistance or hesitation Peter followed. He then came across Andrew and his brother and commanded them to follow Him and they obeyed instantly. This is how the commandant anointing operates. I always wondered how Jesus chose His disciples especially the fact that one could just call people to follow him and they instantly obey but when I got this revelation, it was no more a mystery. Under the commandant anointing, a person even does things that he would never have done if he was not under the anointing. Even if your boss at work would say jump, you would never do it without questioning. This implies that the commanding anointing is beyond any level of authority which an ordinary people of this world can command. It's like the anointing arrests a person and holds him captive to do whatever the minister wants. This type of anointing is usually used to bring demons to submission during a ministerial session to prevent any disorder. The disciples said to Jesus, *"Lord even the demons submit to us"*. However, it could be exercised on anyone who does not have a demon to test the anointing. Due to the power that flows through its commanding nature, a minister operating under this type of anointing can command the dead to rise up and it will be so. Jesus moved in that dimension of the anointing when he commanded Lazarus to come forth and he was brought forth from the dead.

Jesus tapped into this realm of the anointing and rebuked and commanded the waves of the sea to be quiet and they obeyed. As sons of God, this implies that we have power over nature and control of the world. We can command rain to fall and also to stop especially if it's interfering with the work of God. A child of God must not be seen closing his business or ministry on account of bad weather when he can tap into the anointing and do something about it. It is possible to stop rain so that it will not fall only in the territory you are operating at the time. People in other regions where life is going on as usual will continue to submit under nature while you rise above to control it. These are the dimensions which God wants us to tap into Just like Elijah. Jesus said, *"If you say to the mountain be thou removed at be cast into the sea and do not doubt in your heart but believe that those things you say shall come to past, then you shall have whatever.*

According to Benny Hinn, being anointed with authority in the Spirit is a level that is higher and deeper than ministry alone. When flowing in this anointing, your words have the power to plant or uproot. Your words carry weight, and none of your words fall to the ground. Your words have the power to decree and command as led by the Spirit and coming into agreement with and repeating what the Spirit is saying, and speaking under the influence of the Spirit – it's not from the flesh commanding or decreeing things. If it's just the fresh, it will produce no fruit. When you decree and command, then God backs up what you say.

The anointing for authority also involves the area of declaring deliverance to the captives, and the captives are delivered and chains are broken. The anointing for authority involves creative miracles – decreeing and speaking things that are not as though they were, commanding them to be, and it happens just as they say. The anointing for authority involves an anointing for breakthrough. Authority is the kingly anointing – to rule and reign with Christ and know who you are in Christ. To make decrees in the heavenly realms, and it comes to pass. To have authority over demons and Satan, and all powers of wickedness.

Authority also involves taking charge of distractions and people who would mock or cause interruptions in services, which weaken the flow of the Spirit and thus grieve the Holy Spirit. Take charge of any distractions from people hearing the Word, distractions from people hearing the Gospel of Salvation and receiving Christ as Saviour, distractions from people receiving their healing and miracle, and distractions that discourage others in regards to receiving the Baptism of the Holy Spirit or distract the fow of the operation of the Gifts of the Spirit. The anointing for authority involves situations in which satanic plants are sent to churches to try to cause distractions and the demise of the pastors and leadership. On rare occasions, the anointing for authority involves, when directed by the Spirit, pronouncing judgment on those who rise up to try to destroy the work of God, and the Lord backs up your words and He carries out the judgment. An example is Ananias and Sapphira. The apostle Peter and other apostles pronounced a judgment on them not because they lied to them, but because they lied to the Holy Ghost. Another example is when Elijah pronounced a judgment on the young boys who mocked him because of his baldness. He probably was literally bald, but the Scriptures imply that the mocking was deeper than just making fun of his lack of hair, but mocking the anointing on his life.

In the ministry of William Branham, there was a situation that arose in one of the meetings in which he pronounced a judgment by the leading of the Spirit upon a certain man. This man had come up to the stage in the healing line, claiming that he had cancer and for William Branham to lay hands on him so that he would be healed. The man lied – he did not have cancer. His intent was to make a false claim about having cancer, in order to *"expose"* Branham as being a false prophet because he didn't believe that God reveals things to His prophets by the words of knowledge. The man was out to prove that Branham just *"made up"* all those words of knowledge about people. When the man claimed to be sick with cancer, the Holy Spirit told Branham that the man was a fake and was lying, and then Branham told the man in front of everyone there that he lied about having cancer. Then Branham pronounced a judgment on the man for lying not only to him, but to the Holy Ghost, and told him that since he lied about having cancer, that cancer would come on his body immediately and he would be dead by the next day. It happened exactly as what Branham pronounced.

Exercising authority under the anointing also refers to demonstrating the power of God in judgement. Judgment in this case refers to making a judicial decision and pronouncing a verdict and the consequence/ punishment (*if applicable*) according to the laws established by God. The authority to pronounce a judgment is granted to you from a Higher Authority (*God*). The anointing to pronounce a judgment is not the same thing as Matthew 7:1 *"Judge not, lest ye be judged."* In Matthew 7:1, it's not referring to a judicial decision based on right and wrong, but to be critical and despise someone and their shortcomings, and to be very condemning of others, while you yourself are not perfect. This type of judging involves pride – of pointing out the faults of others, while ignoring the plank in your own eye. This type of judgment involves judging others for their actions when you don't know all the facts and have not heard all sides of the story, nor have been in their shoes. This differs from a judgment made by a judge and jury in a courtroom, based on discerning and separating the facts and reaching a verdict. On very rare occasions is a judgment pronounced. The church, as a whole, is not ready for things to go back to the way it was in the early church in Acts. The glory of the Lord has the power to heal and bring about miracles. Yet one can also perish in the glory by things such as irreverence, profaning the holy things of God, doing what Ananias and Sapphira did and so forth.

Practical Demonstration

In a ministerial session, I commanded a young man to jump and he started jumping, to a group of ladies seating on my left I said, *"dance"*, and they started dancing under the anointing. To the young man sitting at the front I said, *"follow me"* and he uncontrollably followed me all over as I moved up and down the aisle like a body guard following his master. To the whole congregation I said, *"laugh"* and they burst out in laughter hysterically. One of these days, I'm looking for every opportunity to make good use of this anointing by commanding rain at my own discretion to fall over certain geographical territories especially those characterised by aridity and also command rain to cease especially in those areas affected by floods.

18. THE EXECUTIVE OR CHARISMATIC ANOINTING

The Bible makes it clear that the things in the realm of the natural are just a shadow or exact representation of the things in the realm of the spirit (Hebrews 11:1). As much as we have people with charisma in the natural, in the realm of the anointing, there is such a thing as *a charismatic or executive Anointing*. This is a covering and governmental anointing. It comes with charisma, dominion and governance and command a high level of power in the spirit realm. In human standards, it could be described as a *Presidential anointing*. It goes beyond the realm of dominion or beyond territorial anointing because of the high degree of maturity and influence in that realm. It is an overseeing anointing. This is the kind of anointing which Moses operated under such that concerning him, God *said I speak to any man through dreams and visions but as for my servant Moses, I speak with him face to face* . This is not just dominion, it is a level beyond that realm. This is the executive anointing at work. This implies that Moses was more than a prophet and more than a minister. The phrase *"face to face"* implies that Moses was part of the executive committee of God. By virtue of his proximity to the Most High God, he automatically became a Board member of Heaven.

God put him at the same level as Him and gave him the same rights as Him and the same mind to engage Him. This is a level beyond callings, gifting and offices because God rebuked Aaron and Miriam who had callings and offices in the capacity of Priests and prophets and told them that while he speaks to them through visions, this was not Moses portion.

Ministers who function under this realm of anointing are highly influential such that anything that they say, the whole world listens. They have a huge influence, global impact and a greater following such that even many pastors follow them. They have matured in the spirit realm and have gone beyond the level of transition from the anointing to glory. They are no longer obsessed with gifting, callings, graces and ministries because they have matured in those realms and now functioning in the realm of love which is the highest realm in God. They have reached what I *call self-actualisation* in God as Abraham Maslow would say in economic language. It is like a kingly anointing which David had. While in the world people exercise their democratic rights to elect kings and presidents, in the spirit realm, God appoints presidents who are anchors of His kingdom. Elijah determined the system of operation of the economy of heaven by shutting and opening Heavens at his own discretion. That is an executive anointing. Joshua fought and commanded the sun to go backwards and God listened to him. That is an executive anointing at work.

Ministers with the executive anointing form part of *the Board of Heaven.* They join the counsel of Heaven for board meetings and have highest decision making powers to determine the outcome and destinies of people, nations and the world in a generation. They engage and negotiate with God and angels just like Abraham pleaded the case of the Israelites with God and he pleaded the case of Sodom and his views were taken into consideration. They represent heaven when on earth and also represent the earth when they are in heaven. They control both the realm of the spirit and physical. They are high level spokesperson of Heaven and represent God at a very high level and whenever something is about to happen either in the world or in the spirit, they are the first to know. Just like Abraham was the first to be notified by God concerning His decision to destroy Sodom. That is why God said that He does absolutely nothing without revealing it to His servants, the prophets. That means, some apostles, prophets, teachers, pastors and evangelists carry this executive anointing. This anointing functions through the law of grace as God chooses his own choice to occupy key positions in the spirit.

19. THE DIAGNOSTIC OR FORENSIC ANOINTING

This is a forensic type of anointing that is used to conduct deep spiritual operations and to examine conditions and cases that are complex, and beyond scientific understanding. It must be understood that each case in the realm of the spirit is unique and requires a different type of anointing to diagnose it. This type of anointing is therefore used to deal with extreme cases which cannot be handled by doctors or medicine. For example, it takes a greater level of anointing to raise someone with fractured bones, amputated limbs or an ICU patient than to cast out a demon. Using this type of anointing, a minister examines a person under spiritual therapy just like a doctor examines his patient. This is a type of anointing which ministers can use to conduct a spiritual operation for complicated sickness and also to mend broken bones, tendons, tissues and to bring back fractured parts of a body together. It also handles complex conditions and extreme cases due to injuries as a result of accidents. This is the type of anointing which ministers use to raise the cripples from the wheel chairs, open the eyes of the blind, open the ears of the deaf and heal diseases. Due to the nature of its operation, it takes a high level of sensitivity to the anointing to tap into this realm.

In this realm of anointing, a person gets to lift up or move objects without necessarily touching them in the physical. For example, a minister can lift up one's hand without touching it. The minister pulls the person ministered to by an invisible hand of the Holy Ghost. If the minister uses the invisible hand to pull him by the legs, the person ministered to will end up falling or shaking on then legs, if he pulls him to the left, the person will move or fall towards the left and if the minister pulls him by the invisible hand in the right direction, he falls to the right, if he uses the invisible hand to pull his whole body, then the whole body will be dragged either forward or backward depending on the direction of the pull. When ministering under this anointing, one can shake the contents in a person's stomach, change the position of the internal organs like a womb, open the womb, speed up the directive system and even control the person's blood pressure. It's like a person is naked right before a scanner and all body parts both internal and external are laid bare before the operator. This anointing gives a minister every single natty gritty details regarding the type nature and number of cells in a body, the organisation or arrangement of atoms, the operation of enzymes and every body system. And gives an insight on how to handle each case. This dimension of the anointing also works in the realm of creative miracles whereby it brings original blue print of body parts when needed. When it deals with cases of demonic possession, it establishes exactly what their operations are and how to burst them out of the body.

53

Practical Demonstration

In my ministry, I have used this anointing to handle very complicated cases like healing internal bleeding, broken fractures and tissues. I read of a man of God called William Brahman whom in his early days of ministry came across a fatal accident where a car can run over a man to such an extent that his skull was fractured and different pieces of the brain were scattered all over the tar. When William Brahman came on the scene, he commanded different body parts and the brains to come together borne to bone, tissue to tissue, tendon to tendon just like Hezekiah commanded the dry bones to come together in the valley of dry bones and the man rose up and walked, Glory to God! This is a high degree of forensic anointing at work. This realm of the anointing can also raise people from the dead.

20 THE BOILING OR LIQUID FIRE ANOINTING

This is the manifestation of anointing in its raw and undiluted state. The anointing feels very hot and its long term effects are felt across a broad spectrum of time, even long after ministering process has ended. It falls like a rain of fire on the congregation, roasting every demonic power present. When it moves, one might think that it is fire yet it's the anointing. When one ministers under this anointing, it feels like a cup of boiling oil flowing through him. Whenever the minister points at a person, he could literally see that oil coming on them. Kenneth Hagin says he *feels* fire in his hands when this anointing comes upon him. The anointing in the palms of his hands burns like fire. When the Lord appeared to him, He touched the palms of his hands with the finger of His right hand, and his hands began to burn as if I were holding a coal of fire in them. It wasn't just warmth— they felt as if they were burning. When this fire jumps from hand to hand then he knows the problem is demonic in origin and all he has to do is cast out the demon and the person would immediately be recovered. This is the same type of anointing which ministers can use to heal incurable sickness such as HIV/AIDS because the HIV virus cannot withstand the acidity of this anointing, hence it is quenched and drenched in the fire.

This is a special and sacred type of anointing that is used for special manifestations such as the raising of the dead. Smith Wigglesworth moved in the realm of boiling anointing when he would drag a dead body from a coffin, point at it and then command it to walk. When Paul says *"the same Spirit that raised Jesus from the dead lives in you,"* he is talking about the manifestation of this type of anointing, it is the one that can get a dead person running. Under this type of anointing, if you command the spirit of a person who has died outside God's will, it comes back with speed because even the power of death cannot afford to detain such a spirit. The departed spirit responds instantly to the call of this type of anointing and becomes too hot in the hands of the power or forces of death. It is liquid fire for liquid results. This explains the spiritual chemistry and the invisible processes of how the dead are raised. The nature of the anointing is such that it is too acidic and highly inflammable such that no devil can stand it even the powers. This is the anointing that was upon Jesus when he went down to Hades and defeated the devil and took away the keys of hell and death. It is used for judgement. Just one drop of this anointing can cause severe damage in the kingdom of darkness. It is like uranium. No demon can hide or create walls of resistance to protect itself from this type of anointing. When demons saw Jesus approaching, they cried out *"Lord Jesus, have you come to destroy us"*, they were actually crying out because of this acidic anointing that they were seeing upon Jesus. At times people cast out demons and they roam about and enter other people but when a minister casts out a demon under this anointing, the demon straight away goes into perpetuity in the lake of fire.

It is the highest level of anointing one can function under. It is this anointing that was in the bones of Elisha and rose a man from the dead almost 400 years after Elisha had died. It is the most acidic spiritual substance in the whole universe. That is why not so many people are able to carry this anointing because they might wreak a lot of havoc and even destroy themselves if they are not careful. The Bible describes the sulphuric nature of the fire that is in the lack of fire but the boiling anointing surpasses that standard in terms of its acidity. It goes beyond the level of destruction. It quenches, it burns, it extinct, it perpetuates. It is like brimstone, like a rain of fire. Unknown to many people, this anointing is one of the spiritual substances that will be used to melt the contents of heaven and earth during the tribulation.

Practical demonstration

In my personal experiences during the course of ministry, sometimes when I minister and the anointing comes, I feel like a cup of boiling oil. Whenever I point at a person, I could literally see that oil coming on them. That anointing has become so permanent in me such that whatever I went I would see a cloud or pillar of fire going ahead of me just above my head like the pillar of fire which led the children out Israel through the wilderness from Egypt.

I have heard of a story whereby certain men were casting out a demon and it was refusing, then they went to report to Smith Wigglesworth and

He said, *"tell that demon that if I come, I must find it gone or else...."* and when they went back and told the demon what Smith Wigglesworth had said, the demon instantly left. This is the dimension of the boiling anointing Smith Wigglesworth taped into. The demon was scared of the acidic nature of the boiling anointing upon his life, hence it preferred to leave than to wait and face the liquid fire and be subjected to perpetuity in the lake of fire. This anointing has power to send demons straight to the lack of fire than to give them room to wonder about.

20. THE PROSPERITY ANOINTING/ FINANCIAL ANOINTING OR ANOINTING FOR WEALTH

This is the anointing to make wealth. Prosperity is God's original Master plan and purpose for humanity. It must be expressly understood that God wants us to prosper and it is His will to prosper financially and materialistically. He wants us to prosper because it is His will. The wealth of the universe belongs to him. Silver and gold is ours. *Prosperity is our birth right.* When the Bible says that, *"It is the Lord who gives us power to create wealth"*, it actually talks about the prosperity anointing because the Greek word for power is, *"Koach"* which refers to an anointing to create wealth. Note that God doesn't give you wealth because he has already given it to you in His redemptive plan through Christ. Instead, he gives you the ability or anointing to bring forth that wealth to you. The Bible records that by faith we are a seed of Abraham and all blessings of Abraham are ours. We are also heirs of the Kingdom, partakers of the divine nature with Christ, financiers of the kingdom, entitled to have access to all the wealth and abundant resources of the kingdom. We have the keys to unlock God's wealth and source of provision. We have been entrusted with knowing the secrets of prosperity in the throne room *God wants us to prosper so that we can effectively and efficiently represent His kingdom in financial matters.* The Calibre of believers which God is raising today is different form the past generations. In view of the times and seasons as specified in the calendar of God, there is a paradigm shift in the realm of the spirit, from a season of ordinary Christianity to a rise of a unique breed of people, a generation of kingdom minded people who shall impact the world for Christ in every sphere of human endeavour though controlling the economic and financial systems of the world, owning banks, estates, running economies, a Joseph generation, an army of kingdom wealth owners and purpose, a Daniel generation, a breed of kingdom governance and impacting the world through godly leadership and influence. Hence, there is an anointing associated or that comes with such a package.

This is the essence of the *prosperity anointing*. It is this kind of anointing that will catapult you to the realm of millionaires. It is the ability to run businesses and make money on behalf of the kingdom. This is the dimension of prosperity in which Isaac operated. The Bible says *Isaac began to prosper and he continued to prosper until he became prosperous (Genesis 26:13).* This implies that there are levels and dimensions in the realm of financial prosperity. However, Isaac migrated from one level to the other until he reached the climax in that realm. This is the same level or realm that many believers shall operate under in these end times as God uses them in the capacity as Kingdom Millionaires.

Practical Demonstration

I laid hands on a someone's bank card (debit Card) which had a zero balance, rebuked the spirit of lack and then commanded money to flow into the card and prophesied saying, *"By this time tomorrow, there will be a lot of money in this account"* and it happened that on the following day the person received a lot of money in her account as I had declared on the previous day. This is the realm of *financial prosperity* which I'm talking about.

On another day, I urgently needed money and did not have any in my account. I had a zero balance, so I inserted my bank card into the ATM machine but there was no money. But then I taped into the anointing for finances and went back went to an ATM and commanded it to release money into my account and the money came out, just like Moses commanded the sea to open up and it listened, Just like Jesus commanded the waves of the sea and they obeyed, just like Joshua commanded the sun to go backwards and it was so. My inspiration was that if all these people across generation did it, how much more I, the new creation with an indwelling presence of the God head, Christ in me the hope of glory!

21. THE BELIEVER'S ANOINTING

The believer's anointing is the measure of the Spirit of God that every believer receives when they are born again. It is placed within the spirit of a believer at new birth. It is the anointing within. That measure of believer's anointing can be increased. It does not remain stagnant. The reasons why it can be increased is No. 1 a believer can grow in faith. It stands to reason that if you can grow in faith, you will grow in the measure of the anointing in your life. So that is one proof why it can be increased. The second reason why it can be increased is that a believer can grow in grace. The Bible says we grow in grace. Grace can be multiplied and grace can increase. And if we grow in grace then we grow in the anointing because grace is tied up to the anointing just as faith is tied up to the anointing. You cannot grow in faith without growing in the anointing. You cannot grow in grace without growing in anointing. They are proportional since they grow together. They are not separated. They are interlinked together. The third reason why the believer's anointing can grow is because of the growth in glory. We are changed and being transformed from glory to glory. And there are different measures of glory right now in this place and all over the world. Every one of us is in different stages of glorification. One day when Jesus comes we will have the fullness of glorification of spirit, soul and body. But right now we all have different degrees of glorification that have taken place in our spirit and in our mind and in our soul and in our body. So a growth in glory produces a growth in the believer's anointing within. The believer's anointing can do certain things. There are certain signs which follow the believer. And these are certain things that every believer who is born again no matter whether they one minute old Christian, one year old Christian, ten year old Christian, they can do the same thing with the believer's anointing.

22. GOVERNMENTAL OR TERRITORIAL ANOINTING

It is an anointing that comes upon an individual to exercise the kind of authority or dominion over a territories or regions. It is based on geographical location. This kind of anointing rests upon those who move in the realm of territorial dominion and is given to enable individuals to govern, rule, reign, enforce, subdue, conquer, and enthrone territories in the realm of the spirit on behalf of the kingdom. Some people have been entrusted with cities, some regions, some nations and some continents and some global visions and depending on the nature of the assignment and the size of the vision, the anointing is appropriated accordingly.

The territorial anointing is therefore that kind of anointing that when it comes upon a man, it enables him to take over new territories for the kingdom, take over countries and the whole world. Its manifestation is evident in men of God who run their ministries at global scale. It gives you greater authority and ruler ship over nations. The Bible says, "*we rule and reign with Christ*". Moreover, it is recorded in Genesis 1:28 *that God gave dominion to man at creation and commanded him to rule, dominate and subdue the earth*. Therefore, this anointing is God's ability given to man so that he can possess territories for the kingdom and subdue the world on behalf of the Kingdom.

Practical Demonstration

One of the visions God has given me is REFOSA (Revival For Southern Africa) which is a regional vision and the type of anointing that has rested on me is such that if I command or issue apostolic and prophetic decrees over this region, things happen exactly as I decree them and by word of knowledge my spirit travels and gets transported hence, I get to know what is happening in these nations Just like Paul said *to the Corinthians church that though I'm absent I'm present with you in the spirit*. Paul governed the churches in Asia in his absentia in the spirit because he had a territorial vision and learnt to tap into the *territorial anointing*. This is because this territory has been entrusted or committed into my hands hence I have the grace to tap into that dimension of the anointing. God will not let you meddle in the affairs of a particular region without you being called to govern it. If you sense that you have unusual interest in a particular city, nation, continent, then its time to find out more from God, maybe you might have a territorial anointing for the particular territory.

23. REPLICATE ANOINTING (ACTION AND REACTION)

This is an anointing that is manifested through *action and reaction or emulation or replication*. In this case, a person upon whom the anointing is administered responds by doing exactly as the minister does in a ministerial context. In other words, He emulates and imitates the minister's actions under the anointing. If the minister waves his hand in a particular fashion, the person will also respond or react by moving in the same direction; if the minister laughs, the person will also laugh, if the minister starts dancing, the person will also dance. The key principle is that whatever the minister does is emulated or replicated by the recipient of the anointing. This is such a powerful anointing because through it, we can impart the power of God upon the masses without necessarily having to convince them to receive.

Just by watching a minister doing something, they can easily receive by emulating his actions. The saying, *"do as I say not as I do"* does not apply in this case because then congregation does exactly what you do and not necessarily what you tell them to do. When Paul says *imitate me as I imitate Christ* (1 Corinthians 11:1), he is actually referring to the *replicate anointing*. In other words, he is making an open invitation for people to tap into this realm of anointing. Moreover, Paul says *brethren consider Jesus the Apostle and High Priest of our confession*. In other words, Paul is saying pattern your life after this man. 1 have seen in many cases people taping into this realm of replicate anointing such that they emulate a man of God, the way he minis-ters the Word and moves in power such that those emulating him function and operates exactly like him. If you keep emulating a man of God long enough, you end up catching his spirit. In this manner, it becomes very easy for people to receive impartation of gifts, graces and blessings from such a man of God when they tap into the realm of replicate anointing.

It is a divine truth that some manifestations are contagious. Saul was not a prophet but when he joined a group of prophets and saw them prophe-sying, then spirit of the Lord came upon him and he started prophesying together with them. If one person catches the anointing, then the rest can follow suit. This is how replicate anointing operates. However, it must be understood that everything must be done in the spirit to avoid a counterfeit replication from the devil. The demon beat the sons of Sceva because they were trying to emulate Paul in the flesh. If they had emulated him in the spirit with power, faith and authority, they would not have fallen in trouble.

However, I have personally had conversations with some folks arguing out that emulation is not right because a person was created unique and should therefore have his own character and not emulate anyone. This is because they have not caught the revelation of how the replicate anointing and its associated blessings flow. And this is the same reason why many are still struggling to receive certain things in their lives. Nothing can be faked in the anointing. There is no such thing as fake anointing. However, there are side effects as bad habits can be emulated when the man of God backslides or does no longer live a holy life.

Practical Demonstration

During a worship service under the anointing, I started singing in the spir-it and instantly everybody started singing in tongues. And when I started laughing hysterically in the spirit, everyone caught the same manifestation and started laughing in the spirit. When I started prophesying, everyone caught the prophetic wave and joined in prophesying. This is how the rep-licate anointing operates.

24. REVELATIONAL ANOINTING

This is a type of anointing that brings forth a deeper revelation of God's word. It opens your understanding of scriptures. It works more or less similar to the accumulative anointing is the sense that one is initially given a measure of revelation and as he uses it, it's like a tap of running water is opened to allow a food of revelation to flow. Unknown to a lot of people, this is the No. 1 grace in the realm of the anointing in that it is a key that unlocks all other realms. Every anointing is provoked or displayed through revelation knowledge. Without revelation, there is no understanding of the flow of anointing, hence no manifestation. Apostles had this grace and it allowed them to write the Bible. In every generation, God raises a man and uses his faculties to document the miracles, and happenings of God in that particular generation. It is through this anointing that Paul wrote the epistles and other prophets were inspired by the Holy Spirit to write the Bible. It is through anointing that one's mind is opened and awakened into the reality of divine truths.

Practical Demonstration

In my ministry, the revelation anointing is the type of anointing that I flow and excel more than any other types. When that anointing comes upon me, a flood of revelations starts flowing in my spirit such that I can continue writing for the whole week day and night without any breaks in between. It is through this anointing that I have managed to write the following collection of over 50 anointed books within a space of less than one year:

> *How to become a Kingdom Millionaire, Deeper Revelations of The Anointing, How to operate in the realm of the miraculous, The Realm of Power To Raise The Dead, A Divine Revelation of The Supernatural Realm, The Prophetic Move of The Holy Spirit In The Contemporary Global Arena, The Ministry of Angels in the World Today, Kingdom Spiritual Laws & Principles, Divine Rights & Privileges of a Believer, Three Keys To Unlocking The Supernatural[The Mantle, The Presence and The Glory], The Prophetic Dimension, New Revelations of Faith, The Dynamics of God's Word, The Sound of Abundant Rain, Times of refreshing & Restoration, The power of praying in the Throne Room, The realm of Glory and Rain of Revelations, a daily devotional concordance comprising of a yearly record of 360 fresh revelations straight from the throne room of God* and many more.

25. SPECIALISED OR ARTISTIC ANOINTING

It is a type of anointing that enables one to execute a specialised task with a high level of artistic skill or excellence. It is *an anointing for excellence*. It causes one to excel at a level far much higher than the rest. You may not be called to the five-fold office, like an apostle, prophet, evangelist, pastor or teacher but as a business man, a professional or a general worker, you could have a special anointing upon your life for your field of work. The Lord may grant you special wisdom and qualification like Aholiah and Bezalel in Moses' days. They were neither preachers nor teachers but they had the skills that came from the anointing upon on their lives. God specially anointed them with those skills. The Sons of Issachar were also gifted in a special way but God and understood the times and seasons of God. This is the artistic anointing at work. Moreover, Mishack, Shadreck and Abednego were tested and found to be ten times more intelligent than their peers. That was the artistic anointing at work. So, the anointing upon is not only belonging to those in the ministry. It's for every believer whatever function and call of ministry that you have God will give you an anointing upon, especially for you in those areas that nobody has functioned in. Whether in the nine ministries of believers or in the five-fold office, you can function to the fullest capacity in your type of anointing that God has upon your life.

CHAPTER TWO

PRACTICAL DEMONSTRATION OF THE NEW WAVES OF THE ANOINTING

The Proliferation Of The New Waves Of The Anointing

26. SUPERNATURAL ANOINTING OIL

This is a transmutation of the anointing from the supernatural realm into a tangible and visible form the natural realm. It is an end time manifestation of the anointing as it changes its form, nature of manifestation and transmutes itself from the spirit realm into the natural realm. In our ministry, we experienced an unusual supernatural occurrence of appearance of oil from heaven which rained down and covered the ceiling of the church and then gracefully dripped or oozed down its walls and eventually soaked the carpet until it became wet with oil. This supernatural oil initially began to saturate and pour out of the atmosphere with the smell of rose. After that it started flowing with the smell of nard. After that it continued flowing out but this time with a new fragrance or smell of myrrh. As if that was not enough, all of a sudden, diamond stones started falling heavily on people's heads during worship like hail stones.

Sometimes as I stand in the glory, my hands and feet will begin to drip with supernatural oil, representing the miracle anointing of God. Many times I will use this supernatural oil to pray for the sick and have seen tremendous healing miracles take place. The supernatural oil that flows from my hands often carries a heavenly aroma – the fragrance of Jesus (Song of Songs 2:1). In Psalm 23:5 David says, *"You have anointed my head with [fresh] oil."* (NASB). God is anointing us with a fresh new impartation from his Spirit! Other times in the glory of God, I have seen tiny sparkles appear in the air or on people. Sometimes the glory will come as a shower of golden rain; sometimes this golden substance will come out from the pores of my skin. I have seen this happen in our ministry on many different people. While praying, a certain woman's hands suddenly became wet with a thin sheen of oil and she began anointing people with it. We found that we could wipe her hands dry, only to have the oil come back just out of her hands. It also was scentless when it was left on her hands but as soon as she anointed people, they could smell it.

27. GOLD DUST ANOINTING

This is the anointing to practically demonstrate the wealth of Heaven on earth through precious stones such as gold dust. A supernatural phenomenon in the realm of God's financial prosperity that has been happening for quite some time now is gold dust appearing on people as a sign of the manifestation of the wealth of heaven on earth and the unveiling of higher realms of God's glory. This wealth of heaven has been manifested supernaturally in divergent ways evidenced by the appearance of gold dusts, silver and diamond stones and supernatural oil soaked on people's bodies, on the ground or on buildings where saints gather for worship. Naturally, there have been strong speculations as to the sources of these phenomena in Christian circles and it seems that the main questions arising about these miracles are firstly what is the source? And secondly what is the purpose? However, it must be fully understood that these are end time manifestations of God's glory. The supernatural manifestation of Gold dust, silver and diamond stones is the most recent wave of glory and prosperity that is sweeping the world. We have been ushered right into the very special divine moments in the calendar of God where we are feeling the first sprinkles of the greatest revival of miracles, signs and wonders ever recorded since the Book of Acts. This is a result of the highest level of concentration of the glory of God being manifested upon the Earth. This wave of revival shall be greater than any other because we are entering the culmination of time, when we will experience the former rains and the latter rains of revival glory combined. Some of the things we are experiencing are familiar, but many things are brand- new. This, too, was foretold in God's Word concerning the last days. A season of exploration and discovery has been ushered as great mysteries are being rediscovered that will unleash the greatest outpouring of God's glory and harvest since the early Church, even since the beginning of time. Therefore, God's golden glory shall bring forth a golden harvest.

The Prophet Isaiah prophesied the following words: *"For behold, darkness will cover the earth and deep darkness the peoples; But the LORD will rise upon you and His glory will appear upon you."* (Isaiah 60:2). Today, this scripture is being fulfilled as the tangibility and visibility of God's glory is grossly manifested upon people. *It must be known therefore that God can and will use whatever He pleases to show himself real to people".* Moreover, God dust represents the wealth of heaven. The Bible declares in Ephesians 1:3 that *we are blessed with all spiritual blessings in the heavenly places and gold dust is a visible and tangible evidence of manifestation of these blessings.* Therefore, the miraculous appearance of gold dust and other precious stones most frequently during times of worship or prayer when hearts are focused on God's splendour and majesty, is a reflection of the spiritual truth that God is majestic and rich in spiritual blessings. Moreover, God declared in Deuteronomy 31:6-8 that *I will never leave you nor forsake you* and these supernatural manifestations are an incontestable evidence that God is with us and when the gold dust manifests itself, this truth is confirmed and our hearts soar in praise of our Royal King who created the universe and can create gold dust, gems, oil, or any other substance. He wishes to give us a glimpse of His power and greatness.

Speaking about the Greater Gory in the end time dispensation, God declared in Hagai 2:8. 7, that *'I will shake all the nations, and they will come with the wealth of all nations, and I will fill this house with glory. The silver is mine and the gold is mine,'* declares the LORD of hosts. *The latter glory of this house will be greater than the former,' says the LORD of hosts.* Note that in the context of the scripture God talks about Gold dust and silver after emphasizing the shaking. In actual fact there are three things which God unveils in this scripture, firstly the *spiritual shaking, then the silver and gold manifestation and lastly the appearance of the glory.* This implies that the manifestation of gold dust is a sign of a great shaking, spiritual awakening and the supernatural move of God. It is a visible and tangible manifestation of God's glory in these end times. When heaven is shaken off, it releases an uninterrupted flow of wealth such as gold dust and silver. In the scripture, God mentions that the glory will be greater. That means there is a connection between gold dust and the glory. This implies that gold dust is a manifestation of the latter glory. In actual fact it is the Glory of God that rains gold dust and diamonds in church. When God said the glory of the latter house shall exceed the former, He actually spoke of these new waves of signs and wonders which shall invade the natural realm in this last dispensation as the masses witness an unusual wave of signs and wonders.

However, God shall continue to orchestrate, manifest and release these new waves of miracles at ever increasing glory. As these precious stones shall continue to fall and oil oozes out supernaturally from the atmosphere, it is as if God is revealing a glimpse of His glory to this church. He is revealing Himself as a supernatural God on behalf of His children while worldly people shall see but not partake of this grace. As ministers across the globe preach on Isaiah 60:2, gold dust, oil and precious stones shall begin to fall

and appear in the hands of many present and shall continue to manifest in greater intensity. It is of paramount significance to emphatically reiterate the divine truth that Gold dust is a sign of God's majesty, wealth and glory present in our lives. It is a spontaneous manifestation of the wealth of heaven on earth. However, some people think it is strange that God would reveal His majesty in this way, but we should try to let God out of the box since He has every right to display His glory and reveal Himself in whatever way He sees ft! The Bible tells us that gold pave the streets of heaven. We think this is amazing, but if God wants to use gold to pave the streets who are we to tell Him that He should use asphalt? When Moses and the elders of Israel went up Mount Sinai they came into the glorious presence of God and the pavement under their feet was made of sapphire. Therefore we should not insist that God does things our way. Philosophically speaking, God doesn't have to use cement and asphalt on His heavenly roads. He can use sapphire, gold, silver or whatever precious stones He chooses. He doesn't have to use human means of communication. We like words. We like pictures. But if God wants to use gold and diamonds and gems to communicate with His children, then who are we to tell Him that He is doing it wrong? Nothing is too difficult for God. We should not be surprised that He is making gold dust and gems appear out of thin air. All He has to do is speak and it is done. But we should praise Him and love Him for choosing extravagant and creative ways to reveal Himself to us. The Bible declares in Job
22:21-25 that,

> *Acquaint now thyself with him, and be at peace: thereby good shall come unto thee. Receive, I pray thee, the law from his mouth, and lay up his words in thine heart. If thou return to the Almighty, thou shalt be built up; thou shalt put away iniquity far from thy tabernacles. Then shalt thou layup gold as dust and the gold of Ophir as the stones of the brooks. Yea, the Almighty shall be thy defence, and thou shalt have plenty of silver .*

This implies that there are also many beautiful and useful elements underground such as gold, silver, gems, coal, and oil which He has created. I don't see it as contrary to His nature throughout the centuries for Him to bestow the actual physical elements of gold, silver, gems, oil or other gifts supernaturally whenever He might choose. The Bible makes it clear that God created everything, God sustains everything and God owns everything. Psalm 104:24 declares, "*The earth is full of your possessions.*" In 1 Chronicles 29:11 we read, "*Yours, O LORD, is the greatness, the power and the glory, the victory and the majesty; for all that is in heaven and in earth is yours.* " Everything in the ground, above the ground, everything in the air, everything that passes through the air ultimately belongs to God. He owns the cattle on a thousand hills, the wealth in every mine. But the truth is it's not ours; it's God's. Wealth is a stewardship from God. So whether it's money, land or possessions, we will never be rightly related to what we have until we recognize that it is not ours. In an endeavour to ascertain the credibility and authenticity of this supernatural phenomenon, these diamonds were taken to experts who analysed and examined them and accordingly declared that the cutting of these stones was so perfect, that they couldn't give them value for the percentage of the diamond stones for there were none like that on earth.

Prophetically speaking, in this end time dispensation there shall be a wide spread global manifestations of gold and silver dust, germs appearing upon people mainly during church meetings. Supernatural oil shall be seen visibly dripping from hands and fingers of people, some of which shall receive gold coins, jewels, gems, diamond or silver. It must be expressly understood that these precious stones are not limited to Gold dust and silver stones only but to other supernatural experiences of other precious stones such as sapphires, topaz, emerald and rubies. In this season, God has sent the angel of precious stones for His people to experience manifestations of diamonds, topaz, emerald, rubies as well as gemstones falling from the atmosphere, inside churches by the hands of angels. The scriptural reference to this supernatural phenomenon is found in Exodus 13:30 where it is recorded that the High Priest wore breastplates adorned with twelve precious stones. Therefore, gold dust, silver and diamond stones are just exactly like the twelve stones of the Ephod, the twelve stones of the twelve tribes of Israel.

Moreover, a heightened degree of angelic activity, visitation and manifestation shall be experienced as believers shall visibly see these beautiful transparent fingers or spiritual beings. However, the degree, intensity and magnitude of manifestation of these spiritual experiences shall all depends on the degree of adoration, level of sensitivity and openness to this spiritual phenomena as well as the depth of worship by believers. However, this phenomenon shall spill over to people's houses, homes and yards, businesses, schools, in the streets and market place as God manifest the visibility and tangibility of His glory to all creation in fullness. In the face of a darkening global economic outlook, God renders a supernatural bail out from poverty, lack and debt and believers shall sell the gems and diamond stones they are receiving supernaturally for money to pay off debts. In the Old Testament the Israelites needed food miraculously. They couldn't have used money at that time as there was no food to buy. So God provided the manna for that time and that need. By the same token, God shall provide gems or gold coins (as some have received) to be sold to buy food or meet our material needs and give us enough to help others whenever He chooses to. Strange as it may sound, we may personally need these items someday soon hence it is best not to limit God in any way. Some of these precious stones shall be sold for a value worthy millions of rands and thus shall create a platform for many believers across the world to be elevated into the realm of kingdom Millionaires.

28. MIRACLE MONEY ANOINTING

This is an anointing to demonstrate miracle money into physical manifestation. Details of the operation of this divine phenomenon have been loaded in one of my books entitled, *"Unveiling the Mystery of Miracle Money"*. In this new wave of signs and wonders many people around the world are beginning to experience money supernaturally appearing in purses, pockets, and bank accounts. Also, instant debt reduction and debt cancellation are increasingly becoming popular as this wave of generosity swells with kingdom wealth. The glory of God is being released in this day with a flow of financial blessing! Paul declared *"I pray that you may prosper in every way and that your body may keep well, even as I know your soul keeps well and prospers."* God has end-time transference of wealth available for you as He is releasing Miracle Money.

The greater truth is that this is the season for Miracle Money. The bible speaks of the Sons of Issachar who had an acute understanding of times and seasons of God hence they knew what Israel ought to do at a time. Specifically it says in 1 Chronicles 12:32 *"from Issachar, men who understood the times and knew what Israel should do—200 chiefs, with all their relatives under their command.* Moreover, the Bible says in Ecclesiastes 3:1 that *"There is a time for everything, and a season for every activity under the heavens."* You may know your season but if you don't know your time, you might act after God has passed by. And it is dangerous for a believer to be standing at a bus stop waiting for God yet God had long passed by. In this season both the times (*Kairos*) and seasons (*Cronos*) have come together marking the climax of highest concentration of God's power. Miracle money is a key characteristic feature of the last wave of prosperity. In Habakkuk 2:2-3 God said, *"Write down the revelation and make it plain on tablets so that a herald[a] may run with it. For the revelation awaits an appointed time, it speaks of the end and will not prove false. Though it linger, wait for it, it will certainly come and will not delay."* This speaks of the end time season whereby believers shall be catapulted into the depths of the miraculous to practically demonstrate Miracles Money. We may want to do things in our timing, but we need to work in accordance with God. A vision waits for an appointed time, but at the end, it shall speak. Likewise, miracle money speaks and cries out for a men or women of faith to tap into the spirit dimension to command it into manifestation. Psalm 102:13 reads, " *Thou shall arise and have compassion on Zion, for it is time to show favour to her; the appointed time has come."* This is indeed the set time to walk in the fullness of the son-ship by practically demonstrating the miracle money grace which God has unreservedly poured upon the body of Christ in this end time season.

Firstly, Miracle Money *is the supernatural manifestation or appearance of money in unexpected places such as people's bank accounts, wallets, bags, pockets or ground without a trace of how it got there in the natural realm.* In the natural, there are divergent types of money and the kind of money one receives is determined by the source it came from. Philosophically speaking, money that come from working is called *"wages"* or *"earned money",* money that comes about when a relative or loved one dies and money is left to the survivors is called *"Inherited Money",* money that comes after winning by chance in a contest, a drawing or even the lottery is called *Chance money.* By the same token, the kind of Money that comes from heaven through supernatural means can only be described as **"Miracle money".** Miracle Money is a special kind of money that God Himself supernaturally releases to His children that trust Him and His Word for it.

Secondly, Miracle money *is a supernatural or divine transference of the original blue print of money from the spirit realm into visible and tangible manifestation in the physical realm under the supervision of angels.* The greater truth is that there is an original blue print of everything that exists in the natural in the spirit realm. In a similar vein, as much as we have money stocked up in banks or in circulation in the economy, there is an original blue print of money in the spirit. When this money is supernaturally transferred and transmuted from the realm of the spirit into the natural realm as a visible and tangible substance, it is called *Miracle Money.* It is a portrait of God's divine intervention in the life of a man's everyday life and need. It is a divine truth therefore that as much as money is a physical form, it is also spiritual. This means that there is an original blue print of money in the spirit and when this money is manifested in the physical realm where it is transmuted into a form that is visible, tangible and feel able, it becomes what we call unusual or Miracle Money. There is a level in which the spiritual crystallises or materialises itself into the natural. *Miracle money is therefore a tangible or direct transference, migration or visible manifestation of spiritual money from the realm of the spirit into the physical realm under the power of the financial anointing.* It must be understood right from the onset that the vehicle for the transportation of this unusual money from the spirit realm into the physical is the work of *angels of finances.*

It is of paramount importance in our understanding of the divine phenomenon of Miracle Money that we clarify the difference between a *blessing* and a *miracle*. A miracle is a supernatural intervention of God in a crisis situation. A blessing is still God's power, but it flows through natural channels. Blessings supersede miracles in that a miracle can be a blessing. However, if you live your life from one miracle to the next, you will live from crisis to crisis. It's better to be blessed with good health than to always need divine healing. God's will is for us to walk in blessing. We all need a miracle at some time to simply jump-start our faith. If it weren't for miracles, we wouldn't grow to the point where we could walk in the blessings of God. Therefore, Miracle Money points us to the blesser who is God. Miracle money is one of those reserved miracles which God is using to bless His people in the end times hence we need to catch a revelation of how to receive it and also demonstrate it to others.

Miracle Money depicts God's sovereign rein and intervention in the lives of people where natural means have failed to make a way. In other words, Miracle Money comes when the natural flow of blessings are stopped or hindered. It is an indication that God in the face of impossibilities will prove Himself strong to those who will trust him and obey His word. The Bible says *Isaac planted crops in that land and the same year reaped a hundredfold, because the Lord blessed him. The man became rich, and his wealth continued to grow until he became very wealthy. He had so many flocks and herds and servants that the Philistines envied him* (Genesis 26:13). Bear in mind Isaac's blessing was released in a time of highly unfavourable economic conditions characterized by a great famine and recession and when his enemies had stopped all methods to assure continued blessing. Isaac's hundred fold release came to him at a time when the devil's crowd had blocked all his methods of increase. By the same token, Miracle money usually comes when things are all stopped up in the natural realm.

The Bible testifies that,

> *The wells that his father's servants had dug in the time of his father Abraham, the Philistines stopped up, filling them with earth And [Isaac] built an altar there and called on the name of the Lord and pitched his tent there; and there Isaac's servants were digging a well* (Genesis 26:25).

In this scripture, we learn THAT our situation is not determined by our environment or surroundings. Your situation is really determined by where you put your belief. What the mind believes, life receives. Therefore, your miracle money will make you a personal witness to the fact that a hundred fold release was not a one-time event that happened only to Isaac in the distant past but a progressive and continuous grace which God freely lavishes upon His children right across generations.

Thirdly, Miracle money *is therefore a divine orchestration of a special grace reserved for the end time dispensation to dispatch, distribute heaven's wealth and financial resources on earth for the purpose of propagating God's divine plans and purpose in the end time season.* In this regard, an open invitation has been made by God through the angels, calling for men and women to step up in faith to freely access the grace which God has reserved for His children. Miracle money is one of those free gifts which God wants his children to partake of in these end times. This is what the Bible describes as Buying without money Jesus said;

"Hey there! All who are thirsty, come to the water! Are you penniless? Come anyway—buy and eat! Come, buy your drinks, buy wine and milk. Buy without money—everything's free! Why do you spend your money on junk food, your hard-earned cash on cotton candy? Listen to me, listen well: Eat only the best, fill yourself with only the finest. Pay attention, come close now, listen carefully to my life-giving, life-nourishing words (Isaiah 55:1).

People tend to ask a question: *"Can God give anybody money without working for it?"* Emphatically, Yes. He can because He is revealing unto us His key and integral role as the father who cares for His children. Miracle money is given by God free of charge, even without working for it or paying for it or doing anything but it's a manifestation of God's grace as a way of showing love and care to His people.

29. CREATIVE MIRACLE ANOINTING

There is another type of anointing called *creative miracle anointing* which involves the ability to function in the realm of creative miracles. This is the anointing for creative miracles. It is released specifically to launch believers into greater depths of the miraculous. A creative miracle *is an impartation of a completely brand new organ or body part upon an individual who previously did not have it in existence.* It is a creative miracle in the very sense of the word; to create means to bring forth into manifestation or existence something that was previously not there. It is therefore a creative miracle in the sense that an organ did not exist at all in the body but now a brand new one has been imparted from Heaven. However, creative miracles don't only occur on human bodies but on non-living objects as well. If a broken car comes into contact with God's power such that it starts functioning smoothly, then a creative miracle would have happened.

Examples of creative miracles are: the creation of flesh and bones where there was previously nothing, the growth and infilling of new gold teeth, appearance of hair on bold heads, supernatural appearance of miracle money in people's ac-

71

counts, wallets or bags, instantaneous supernatural loss of weight as well as the appearance of eyes, hands, legs and other body parts in areas where there was completely nothing, a short person getting tall instantly, instant development of a pregnancy evidenced by a growth of a big tummy, giving birth to a baby within three days of pregnancy are all creative miracles.

The rationale behind creative miracles is that there is an original blue print of every body part in heaven's power house such that in the event that someone loses one of his body parts due to accident, misfortune or complications at conception or birth or any calamity of life, their parts can be instantly reinstated, imparted or restored to their original position of normal perfection. It should therefore be understood that in heaven there is a power house that consists of an original blue print of all body parts where one can tap into the realm of power to command that specific body part to be imparted upon an individual who has a missing organ in his body. I'm not talking about a situation whereby God restores a body organ to its proper function but a case where God creates something that was completely not there. In a practical sense, one could command a person's left hand to shorten and be pushed back in Jesus' Name to conform to the person's original blueprint found in heaven. For example, if God has created you to be 5 feet 10 inches, and you are slightly deformed and are only 5 feet 7 inches, then under the anointing of the Holy Spirit, one can command your backbone to be straightened up and reach your ideal height according to the blueprint God made you to be. However, one cannot pray that you grow to be 8 feet because that is not your original blueprint in heaven. Prophetically speaking, taking into account the nature of this end time dispensation, God wants us to migrate or graduate from the realm of ordinary miracles to the realm of creative miracle

CHAPTER TWO

DEMONSTRATING THE FLOW OF THE ANOINTING USING PROPHETIC GESTURES OR BODY MOVEMENTS

Prophetic Gestures are powerful in the realm of impartation or flow of the anointing. This is because they are used to demonstrate the ac tions of faith when operating in the realm of the anointing. The gesture that you display will determine the nature, level, amount and volume of the anointing to be imparted at a particular time. Each gesture produces a different flow and manifestation of the anointing. The use of different gestures depends on the type of assignment or ministry undertaken. For example, casting out of demons requires the use of different gestures than blessing the masses. The use of some gestures is also determined by the speed with which work has to be executed. For example, a finger cannot accomplish much as compared to a use of a shadow or wave. This anointing flows through heavenly sounds such as clapping, shouting, or waving. Heavenly sounds provoke the flow of the anointing and causes all heavens' attention to be directed towards the place where the anointing is practically demonstrated.

30. THE WAVING ANOINTING:

"The anointing demonstrated through Stretching or waving Hands"

This type of anointing works through the power of lifting hands. In other words, it is channelled through the waving of hands. It is recorded in Exodus 17:11-16 that when the Israelites were fighting against the Moabites, as long *as Moses' hands were up, Israel was wining but as he dropped his hands, they were losing.* This scripture unveils the secret of the *waving anointing.* Moreover, the Bible unveils a very interesting account in which the children of Israel faced the surging waters of the sea and then cried to the Lord but then God interrupted them and said, *"Why are you crying to me? What is it that is in your hands? Stretch forth your rod towards the sea and your way will open up"*. The Bible says Moses stretched his hand and the waters of the red sea were divided. This was a live and practical demonstration of the *waving anointing* . It is called a waving anointing because it is channelled through the waving of hands. A hand is a point of contact with divinity. It is a symbol of God's power and a divine instrument to administer the anointing. Therefore, as you wave your hand towards the congregation, you send signals in the realm of the spirit that compels all forces of divinity to act in the direction of your wave. In a practical sense, when demonstrating the waving anointing, a minister stretches his hands towards the congregation and shouts, "Holy Ghost touch!", *"Take it"* , *"Receive the anointing"* , *"Power of the Holy Ghost"* or whatever utterance the Holy Ghost grants him. At the wave of hands, an overflow anointing starts flowing like a food of rain upon the masses result- ing in them falling under the power. As a minister waves his hands towards the congregation, the anointing flows from him through the waves of the air to saturate their bodies with the rain of the anointing. In some cases the waving of hands can provoke the flow of the anointing even without any word uttered.

There is something that happens in the realm of the spirit when we lift hands. The power of God is provoked to erupt like a volcano, causing an explosion in the spirit world. Lifting or waving of hands is such a powerful prophetic gesture that sends signals in the spirit, alerting all spirit beings that heavens' authority is being exercised on the scene.

When the disciples of the early church gathered for prayer and called on the name of the Lord saying, *"O, Lord, stretch forth your hand to perform mir- acles, signs and wonders"*, the Bible says the place where they gathered, was visibly shaken by the power of God (Acts 4:30). This is to show you how powerful it is when God stretches forth His hand. Therefore, as sons of God, when we demonstrate the same actions of faith as God does, there is a shaking, quaking and stirring that takes place in the spirit realm. David understood this principle hence, he proclaimed *"lift up your hands yee gates and be lifted up yee everlasting doors* (Psalms 24:7). Whenever the Bible speaks about the hand of the Lord or the arm of the Lord being stretched, it speaks of the demonstration of power *(anointing)*. Therefore, as custodians of God's anointing, when we stretch or wave our hands, we tap into the realm of God and do whatever God can do. This is because God demonstrates His actions of faith and produces results, hence, we can also demonstrates the same actions of faith to obtain the same results as God. When Elijah prayed, he saw a cloud as small as a man's hand, representing the move of the spirit and the rain of God's power. The cloud assumed the shape of the hand of man because a man's hand is a symbol of God's power. It is an instrument of God's glory. It is a point of contact with divinity. That is why just by greeting and shaking hands with people, the anointing is transferred and blessings transacted. I have observed in my ministry that as I begin to prophetically declare *"My hands are not my own hands, my hands are a symbol of God's power, my hands are an instrument of God's glory"*, I literally feel the power of God flowing out of my hands. In that atmosphere of the anointing, when I start waving my hands towards the congregation, people fall under the power liker the scattering of leaves under the influence of a storm.

Practical demonstration

I recall vividly when I used to pray a lot with my hands folded or dropped down until the day the Holy Ghost literally lifted up my hands during a prayer session. I watched as my hands were carried up into the air. The feeling was so remarkable that from that day onwards I caught a revelation of the power of waving hands. Acting on that revelation, in one of our meetings, I casually waved my hands towards the congregation and shouted, *"Holy Ghost Touch!"*, *"Receive the power of the Holy Ghost"* and at the wave of my hands, an unprecedented rain of the anointing was released from the Heavens' Power House such that when it fell upon the masses, they were flung backwards, scattering the chairs all over the place. It was as if all taps of heaven had been opened to provoke such an unprecedented flow of the anointing. It was as if God Himself was marching His feet over the auditorium. That wave of the anointing left an unmistakable imprint of the Divine stamped on everyone who attended that meeting.

31 .THE POWER SHOUT / VOCAL ANOINTING

"Demonstrating the anointing through Shouting"

This type of anointing is transferred through *voice or vocal sounds*. It is activated through shouting as one of the most significant heavenly sounds. It must be understood that a greater measure of the anointing is provoked through heavenly sounds such as *shouting, clapping, singing, screaming* and so forth. The principle is that at the sound of one's voice, the anointing is provoked to flow instantaneously on the scene. It can go as far as one's voice goes and as loud as the voice is heard. This is the realm of anointing which Peter functioned in at the house of Cornelius. The Bible records *that as Peter began to speak the word, then Holy Ghost fell upon all those who heard the word* (Acts 10:1). This implies that the anointing was transferred through the sound of

Peter's voice. Only those who heard his voice received the anointing and those who did not hear it, received nothing. The fact that the Bible makes it explicitly clear that the Holy Ghost fell upon all them that heard the word tells me that Paul must have shouted at the loudest sound of his voice. If he had whispered, only a few would have heard him and the anointing would have trickled. But the fact that it mentions the Holy Ghost falling mightily upon the masses means that multitudes must have heard Peter's voice as he shouted the word. This is similar to the *resurrection anointing* that was activated at the tomb as Jesus shouted, "Lazarus, Come forth!" And the man who had been in the grave for four days, came out alive. This is the operation of *the Vocal anointing*. This is to tell you that there is power in shouting. That is the secret of provoking the anointing. David understood this dimension hence he says *"Shout to the Lord you all earth"* (Psalms 98:4-9).

The power of God is manifested through miracles, signs and wonders as people shout. Shouting sends electrifying signals in the realm of the spirit and has the power to change the prevailing atmosphere. As people shout, *"Jesus!", "Fire!", "Power!", "Hallelujah!", "Amen!"* or whatever utterance the Spirit grants them, they provoke a stirring and a shaking in the spirit. It is recorded in (Acts 4:31) that when the disciples lifted up their voices unto God, meaning when they shouted and said *"O, Lord, you who created the heavens and earth. Stretch forth your hand to perform miracles, signs and wonders",* the place where they were meeting was shaken. The key to their breakthrough was in shouting. It is the shouting that provoked the shaking. The secret is in shouting. It is a shout that brought down the walls of Jericho. At the sound of their voice, the walls of Jericho fell under the power. This is to tell you that the same power that brought the walls of Jericho down is the same power that makes multitudes of people to fall under the power during ministerial sessions. At times we are not aware of the impact of the words of faith that we release in the spirit realm when we shout to God. This is what happened in the invisible realm when the children of Israel shouted at the wall of Jericho: Their voices mingled with faith from their spirit, joined the breath of the Holy Ghost and went through the air like fiery darts, piercing through the corridors of the spirit world and casing an explosive spark which was then exerted on the wall of Jericho in the natural realm and caused it to fall under the power. This is to tell you that as we shout and sing praises unto the Lord, the walls of limitation in our lives are brought flat down. The strongholds of evil in our lives are dismantled and any walls of resistance in our families, finances, ministries and businesses are demolished. Unknown to multitudes of believers, this is just how powerful shouting is as a heavenly sound.

The question that you are probably asking yourself is: Why did God command the children of Israel to shout at the wall of Jericho? While in the natural realm, shouting might not have made any sense or significant impact, in the realm of the spirit, that was actually a demonstration of faith. God needed them to release something from their spirit that could be used as a point of divine contact for Him to release His power. Through the act and heavenly sound of shouting, the children of Israel released substantial spiritual material which angels used to manufacture a spiritual substance that was then used to bring the walls of Jericho down. You see, God needs material to work with in order to release your breakthrough. As the children of Israel they released the manifestation though a shout, heaven released the corresponding divine energy to set it in motion.

The walls of Jericho crumbled because people shouted— another amazing defiance of the law of gravity. What made the walls fall? The Israelites were told not to speak for one week. In this way they were conserving the power of the sound in their voices so on the day they released it their shouts would have greater power. Words and sound contain certain levels of energy. If you say "In the name of Jesus" with a tired voice, after having talked all day about nonsense, the power of your words is weakened. On the other hand, if you spend the day meditating on God and then speak, there is power in your words. Imagine the Israelites spending an entire week not talking or being distracted or speaking negative words. The entire time their minds and spirits were preoccupied with God and with the anticipation of what He would do next. Then finally, after conserving all their sound waves, on His command, they together released one big shout and shofar blast— the power was like a sonic boom. Sounds waves full of glory and power like a laser were concentrated on the walls around the city of Jericho— and down they came. I believe the walls were overpowered by the stream of concentrated sound waves emanating from the people's shouts, which blew out all the sound waves in the rocks. Because the rock wall was essentially made of the building block of sound and it was bombarded with greater sound waves of glory coming from an army of God's people, the wall crumbled as the very element that held it up was shattered.

It has been scientifically proven that if a person sings at a very high pitch long enough, glass will break—break— especially a fine crystal goblet. The sound pierces right through the glass, which is also made of sounds, and shatters it. A jet aircraft traveling faster than the speed of sound causes things on earth to shake because of the great power of the sound waves. In November 2005, a cruise ship was attacked by pirates in the waters near Somalia. The ship's crew used a newly developed nonlethal weapon that sends out high-powered air vibrations. They aimed a sonic sound boom at the pirates who were trying to board the ship, and the blast knocked them off their feet. Fortunately, the cruise ship out-maneuvered the pirates and moved out into deeper waters. 2 Can you imagine sounds loaded with the glory and power of God? There is a sound of God's glory that is released when we shout to the Lord corporately. As mentioned previously, sound is also energy and matter and it has energy and weight to it. Sound is a non-visible element but a very real object that, when in a concentrated form and filled with His glory, is a force to be reckoned with.

Do you remember the account of how multitudes welcomed Jesus during His triumphal entry in Jerusalem by shouting and singing praises? (Luke). Do you remember what Jesus said to the Pharisees and rulers when they ordered the people to keep quiet? He said, *"If these people keep quiet, these very stones will cry out"*. Wow! Imagine the stones crying out and singing praises to God! This is to tell you that Jesus legally endorsed *shouting* as a key heavenly sound that we should use in worshiping our God. If shouting didn't have any significant impact in the spirit realm, Jesus would not have endorsed it all. This tells me that there is something remarkable that shouting does to the spirit man. Shouting stretches the capacity of the human spirit, making it larger, broader, more open for the torrential rain of the anointing to flow through.

Practical demonstration

During a ministerial session, in one of our services, I commanded everybody in the congregation to raise their expectancy level to receive the anointing. I then declared that as I count from one, they should shout, "Jesus!" until the third time and an *overtaking anointing* will flow upon them like a food of waters. As I led them in the very act of activating the anointing, the minute they shouted, "Jesus!" for the third time, everybody in the congregation fell under the power, with some screaming, rolling and laughing hysterically in the spirit. Others testified that as we shouted the Name, "Jesus!", they heard the voice of Jesus Himself commanding the demons in them to come out. Besides, divergent manifestations and operations of the Spirit were evident; having been provoked by the act of shouting the name of Jesus!

During one of our deliverance sessions, on a different occasion, under the directorship of the Holy Spirit, I asked the congregation to shout, *"Fire!"* seven times and as they acted on that revelation, Heavens' Power House released the fullness of God's fire such that even the physical atmosphere became terribly hot hence, even the worst demons could not withstand it. They manifested violently and instantaneously came out of their victims without anybody laying hands on them. Others testified that as we shouted

,"Fire!" they felt that our voice were amplified such that they heard them as the sound of thunder echoing through the spirit world. Wow! This is the essence of operation of the *vocal anointing*. It is transmitted through Heavenly sound.

32. THE POWER CLAP ANOINTING
Demonstrating the anointing through Clapping

This type of anointing is provoked by the sound of clapping of hands. While stretching forth hands sends signal in the spirit, clapping hands is a symbol of clash of powers in the realm of the spirit . This is why in the demonic realm, some people manipulate this dimension such that if they want people to fight, they could just clap or bring both hands together with power and chaos will instantly manifest upon their victims in the natural realm. There is a signal of power that is released in the realm of the spirit by reason of clapping hands. It is a sign of acknowledging God for the display of His power. Clapping of hands is one of the divine strategies by which we reinforce the victory of the Lord Jesus Christ over the devil *as He made a public spectacle of him, triumphing over him by the power of the cross*. It is a symbol of certifying or reinforcing victory in a similar fashion in which sports fans clap their hands throughout the game as a sign of assurance of victory for their teams.

Therefore as believers clap their hands, that sound of victory causes commotion, chaos or confusion in the enemy's camp as it reminds the devil of his fatal defeat by the Lord Jesus Christ on the cross. Such a prophetic action undeniably renders him powerless , impotent and completely out of action. Clapping is a means of praising God and *as His praises goes up to heaven, His glory and anointing rains heavily upon multitudes in the natural realm.* David understood this realm hence, he commanded people everywhere to *clap their hands* (Psalms 47:1). There is a secret behind clapping hands. There is an uninterrupted flow of the anointing that is triggered by the clapping of hands. When Jesus entered Jerusalem in royalty, multitudes welcomed him by clapping, shouting and making the loudest noises. When the Pharisees asked Jesus to order the people to keep quiet, that was actually Satan himself speaking through them because that noise was causing a shaking in the demonic realm and wreaking havoc in his kingdom. This is to tell you that clapping is a warfare tool. As we clap our hands with revelation, sparks of lightning are released into the spirit world, scattering the powers, principality and agents of Satan, thus, restoring God's order in the spirit realm.

Practical demonstration

During a ministerial session, a demon interrupted me by manifesting and making noise. I was provoked in the spirit and then commanded everybody in the congregation to clap their hands unto the Lord. As they did, the anointing of God broke loose and thrashed the demon and with a loud cry, it instantly departed. It was as if something was loosed from the spirit like the gushing down of a wave. In this case, the demon kept quiet under interrogation. Firstly, they hope to escape by pretending not to be there. Secondly, this is the devil's strategy to counter the vessel's judgment of him. Thirdly, they do not want you to know their secrets.

33. THE POWER KICK ANOINTING

Demonstrating the anointing through Kicking

The power kick anointing is transferred or channelled through a prophetic action or gesture that involves moving one's legs in the direction of the person being ministered to as if the minister is actually kicking him. In this demonstration, the minister actually uses his legs as a point of contact to transfer the anointing to its intended recipients. It can be effectively used especially during deliverance services to kick and bust out devils. This kind of anointing operates in the same way as the power shot anointing. The difference is that in the case of *power kick anointing*, a legs are used instead of a finger. The greatest advantage of this action of faith is that it can exert a lot of pressure or release greater power, divine energy or spiritual force that can send devils flying in the air before they are busted out. This type of anointing is rarely used in the church because during ministerial sessions, we use more of our hands than legs to administer the anointing.

The use of legs during ministration is not a widespread action of faith because nowhere in the Bible does it talk about the laying on of legs. Instead, more emphasis is always placed on the laying on of hands. However, be that as it may, it must be understood that it's not only our hands that are anointed but our legs as well. Understand that your spirit is not only in your hands; instead, it assumes the shape of your body hence, as you demonstrate your actions of faith through power kicking, it is actually your spirit that is performing the task and touching the one who is being ministered to. In a spiritual sense, as you demonstrate that prophetic gesture, demons actually don't see you kicking. Instead, they see your spirit attacking and thrashing them. At times when you release a power kick, the person does not fall backwards; instead, he is first flung upwards in the direction of the kick before he could land on the ground. This is why I strongly advise that this action of faith be used when one is busting devils, especially stubborn ones. The Bible makes it clear that all demons are under your feet. Therefore, by demonstrating your actions of faith through power kicking, it's actually a way of establishing that truth in the spirit realm and keeping the devil where he belongs – right under your foot.

Practical demonstration

During another ministerial session, a demon started manifesting in a young man rhythmically. I was provoked in the spirit, and expelled the demon by saying, *"All your legal rights are stripped. Go in Jesus' Name to the place of wrath assigned to you."* I then swayed my leg as if I'm kicking the air in the direction where the young man was standing and as I did that, he flew several metres into the air and coming down with a thud, the demon instantly came out of him. I then explained "When I say, *"All your legal rights are stripped,"* this means that the demon has no more right to make petition to defend himself since he would have defied the Holy Spirit and violated the spiritual laws of heaven. There are rules in heaven for demons to behave too. They cannot overstep the limits permitted by God. If they do so, they are instantly judged and consigned to hell before their time.

CHAPTER FOUR

DEMONSTRATING THE FLOW OF THE ANOINTING USING BODY PARTS

It is a divine truth that God uses our bodies as a point of contact to flow and touch those that we minister to. That is why the Bible says *our bodies are a temple of the Holy Ghost* (1 Corinthians 6:19). Now, ask yourself this sober question: What is the temple used for? It's a place of worship and ministration of the anointing. By the same token, your body is used as a pipeline or divine instrument to administer the anointing to its intended recipients. Note that during ministration, God does not bypass you to touch those that you minister to in your sphere of contact. Instead, He uses your body as an arch to transfer the anointing upon others. However, He touches your spirit first and that anointing is then assimilated from your spirit into your body which would be used as a vehicle to demonstrate the anointing. This is the realm I call the *vessel anointing* because a vessel is used as a channel to bring about the flow of the anointing. At times the anointing is displayed through eyes, hands, shadow, breath, legs and so forth. The demonstration of each anointing is unique hence the manifestation is also different. In other words, each body part brings a different flavour and colour to the type of anointing manifested. For example, a hand can administer a specific anointing that is different from what a leg or eyes can minister. The following are various types and manifestations of the anointing which fall under this category:

34. THE EAGLE VISION OR EYE SIGHT ANOINTING

Demonstrating the Anointing through the Vessel's Eyes

This is a type of anointing that is released through the eyes of a human vessel. I call it an *eagle vision anointing* because a minister is able to see right into a person's thoughts, motives, feelings, attitude or situation using the sharp eye of an eagle. In the same way an eagle surveys land from a distant, through this anointing, one is able to scan and detect problems and establish the root cause of situations and circumstances from afar. This type of anointing is introspective or interrogative in nature. It excavates mysteries and exposes hidden things which man would never have known under ordinary circumstances. It gets to establish the bottom of the matter, the root cause of the problem, in terms of how it started, why and how it should be best dealt with. Demons that possesses the faculty of a person and are hiding behind their souls, emotion and will can no longer hide but are exposed by this type of anointing. The anointing that flows through a vessel's eyes is so powerful that it releases or radiates the power straight into the spirit, soul and body of a recipient. For example, demons screamed whenever they saw the Lord Jesus Christ because of the anointing that was flowing from Him. Kathryn Kuhlman was also known to stare at people such that they few under the power coming from her eyes. It is said that in her encounter with a certain lady in one of her meetings, the moment the lady's eyes collided with those of Kathryn Khuhlman, a powerful force thrust her backwards and she backpedalled uncontrollably to the end of the hall where she collapsed on the floor. She later testified to the congregation she felt a powerful force from vessel's eyes hitting her lungs such that she felt energized, powerful and rejuvenated.

The Bible records an incident in Acts whereby Peter and John met a crippled man at the Beautiful Gate of the temple and peter asked the man to look at them intently. The question is: Why did peter demand that the man look at them? Besides drawing the attention of the man in the direction of the healing anointing, staring at them was actually a prophetic gesture to transfer the anointing from his eyes into the crippled man. Peter actually tapped into the law of impartation by point of contact to give birth to an instantaneous healing in a man. As the man gave them attention by staring at Peter, the anointing flowed from his body through his eyes into the body of the crippled man , quickened him and raised him up. Do you remember how Elisha received an impartation of the prophetic anointing from Elijah? It was though eye sight. Howe do I know that? Because Elijah said to Elisha shortly before impartation, *"If you could only see me when I'm taken up, it's all yours"*. And the fact that Elisha later got that anointing means that he must have seen Elijah as he left for heaven. As he saw him, he received the anointing.This is to tell you how powerful a vision is because in the realm of the spirit, things are possessed by sight or through vision. The moment you see it, it becomes yours. That is why part of demonstrating this anointing can involve asking a member of the congregation to read a portion from an anointed book or from the Bible and as they do that, the anointing flows form the book through their eyes right into their bodies causing them to fall under the power. Prophetically speaking, as you are reading through this book right now, the anointing that is loaded and captured in the pages of this book is literally flowing into your body through your eyes. As you are reading through, you are literally absorbing the anointing into your spirit such that you will begin to demonstrate it even before you could finish reading this book.

Practical demonstration

During a service, I randomly handpicked a young man and called him to the front. I then asked him to quickly look into my eyes. He screamed and fell to the floor. When he got up, he went to the mike and testified to the congregation, "*When I looked into Apostle Revelator's eyes, I saw they were like balls of fire. Some bright laser light shot out from his eyes and entered into my body and I saw some black shadow instantly leaving me.*" I then told the congregation, "When I say, '*Look at me,*' you must make an effort to look at my eyes immediately, otherwise you will miss a doze of the anointing." After drawing the attention of everybody, I looked up and said to the congregation, "*Everybody, Look at me.*" Everyone in the congregation quickly looked at my eyes and instantly they received an impartation like an electric shock such that they started coughing violently as demons were expelled from them. Others testified that the instant they stared at my eyes, they saw a flame of liquid fire coming towards them such that it overwhelmed their spirit and brought forth instantaneous healing and deliverance in their bodies.

During another ministerial session, under the directorship of the Holy Ghost, I called out saying, "*Somebody on the right side of the congregation is having a chest problem. You are feeling very hot and uncomfortable in your chest.*" Somebody that fits the description stood up and went to stand in the middle of the aisle. I then said to him, "*A doze of the anointing will rain on you the instant I look at you.*" The moment I looked at him, he let out a scream and fell under the power. Later, he came to the mike and testified, "*I saw fiery power coming from the Apostle's eyes such that I received an immediate relief in my chest.*"

During a deliverance session in one of our meetings, I looked at the congregation and authoritatively commanded all demons to come out of the people. As I communicated that decree, demons instantly left them. Many in that meeting came out to testify that as they looked at my eyes, they saw a bright offensive light emanating from my body whose heat felt hotter than the sun. Others confessed that when they looked into my eyes, they actually didn't see me but they saw Jesus inside me hence, demons could not stand in His presence but came out instantly.

35. POWER POINT ANOINTING OR FINGER POINT ANOINTING

"Demonstrating the Anointing through A Finger"

The anointing demonstrated through the finger overlaps with that displayed through the glory finger. The working is different. The glory finger is through the Glory of God. This is one of the most powerful demonstrations of the anointing because the figure is very specific – it will always point you in the direction of the problem, making it easier for a solution to come forth. This finger anointing literally points the finger at the root problem. The healing through the finger operates in this manner: A person with a heart problem may have 5-6 symptoms. The root problem is in the heart. The finger anointing points to the root problem and once the heart problem is healed, all the symptoms and side effects will disappear. Even indirectly related problems will disappear. This anointing must be directed by the Holy Spirit in order for it to be administered effectively.

Another peculiar manifestation of this type of anointing is what I call a *shot gun anointing*. In this case, a minister demonstrating this anointing folds his hand into a fist while at the same time stretching forth two of his fingers such that his hand looks like a gun. When he points at a sick or demon possessed person, in the spirit realm, bullets of power or anointing are released to the extent that some people testify that they actually saw real bullets being shot directly at them at that time when that anointing was administered. What people see in the natural realm as a simple folded hand with two outstretched fingers is actually seen as a machine gun – a weapon of mass distraction in the realm of the spirit.

Practical demonstrations

During a ministerial session in one of our services, I received a word of knowledge and then called out *"There is a person with a heart condition in this place. You have general weakness over your body. You are experiencing heaviness in your heart. Your leg movement is also slow. You feel sleepy and tired all the time."* A woman stood up and claimed all the conditions. I then pointed my finger at her, and she ran backwards the full length of the aisle, screaming at the top of her voice uncontrollably, before falling under the power. The finger anointing is very powerful. It had blasted away the evil spirits that are causing these physical problems to her. The evil spirits were immediately sucked out by the anointing. After she got up, she went to the mike and testified, *"I saw a ball of fire coming from Apostle Revelator's finger. My whole body was set on fire. I could perceive some dark forces outside blasted away. I feel very light in my feet, legs and heart. All glory and thanks be to God."*

36. THE SHADOW OR REFLECTIVE ANOINTING
"Demonstrating the Anointing through a Shadow"

Do you know that a shadow can be used as a vehicle to demonstrate the anointing? The truth is that the anointing is not only limited to the pages of the Bible- it does not only flow through people's bodies, handkerchiefs and aprons only. It can also flow through a shadow or any reflection of light by an object. This is the same anointing which Peter taped into during the days of the early church when multitudes brought the sick and laid them on couches and beds so that at least the shadow of Peter passing by might fall on some of them. (Acts 5:15). The anointing had so much soaked into Peter and flooded his spirit and such that it permeated the core and every fibre of his being, assimilated into every cell of his blood and infiltrated every bone of his body such that it began to ooze out and was automatically reflected and radiated through his shadow. Isn't it amazing that the anointing of God even flowed through a shadow? We all know that a shadow has no natural materiality yet God's power flowed wherever the shadow of Peter was reflected. What is the explanation for that? The Bible says, *"Christ in me, the hope of Glory"*, meaning that Christ is the glory of God resident in our spirit. Therefore, a shadow was actually an outward reflection of the glory of God in Peter's spirit. The glory of God had to flow from within him and God chose to use a shadow to reflect or radiate the glory to touch lives. So, the anointing had to flow through a shadow because the anointing is what connects you to the glory. Note that it doesn't say that all the sick were healed by Peter's shadow but it says some of them were healed. Why? Because only those who lay in the direction of the shadow were rightly positioned to receive their healing.

Philosophically speaking, the shadow of Peter operated in the realm of the spirit like a mechanism or key that supernaturally opened all doors. It worked like an automatic door. There are three times of doors in the natural realm. The first one has a handle; if you lock it and throw away the key, you can't open. The second door uses a code; in order for you to open it, you need a code to match the number and it opens. Without a code you can't open. But there is another door called the automatic door. With this one, you don't need a key or a code to open it, it just detects your image as you approach and it opens on it's own accord. In the realm of the spirit, the shadow of Peter operated like an automatic door. As it came into contact with the sick, they were healed and as spiritual doors saw the shadow approaching in the spirit, they started opening up on their own accord. This is the realm of the *shadow or reflective anointing*.

Practical demonstration

During a ministerial session at one of our conferences, I felt a Holy Ghost prompting to demonstrate the shadow or reflective anointing so as to strengthen believers' faith in the power of God. I first located my shadow and made it a point that it became visible to everyone as it got reflected by light. I then randomly called two groups of people from the congregation; those who were sick and those who were afflicted by demons, to come and stand on the stage. I then passed by, making sure that my shadow was reflected in the direction where they were standing. Strikingly, as their bodies came into contact with my shadow, they all fell under the power and as they rose from the ground, those who were sick were all healed and those who were oppressed by demons were instantly delivered. I'm certainly sure that there was an unmistakable imprint of the Divine stamped on everyone who came into contact with my shadow that day, glory to Jesus!

Using a different demonstration, I touched the wall of our building with my hand and then asked the congregation to locate the shadow of the building. Being sure of the direction in which the shadow of the building was reflecting, I then asked everybody to go and stand right in the middle of the shadow. As they did, they all simultaneously fell under the power. Those who were sick were healed and many received alarming breakthroughs in their lives. This is to tell you that as a minister, you don't have to exhaust your body by laying hands every time you want to impart or minister to the sick and the oppressed. There are a *rhapsody of demonstrations* that you can pioneer in your ministry that can culminate in multitudes being healed and delivered at the same time without any physical effort.

37. HAND SHAKING ANOINTING

"Demonstrating the Anointing through the shaking of hands"

There is something about the handshaking anointing that believers across the globe have not yet comprehended. Did you know that in the realm of the spirit, a hand is such a vital tool in the demonstration of the anointing? It is actually a symbol of God's glory and an instrument of God's power. God uses your hand as a point of divine contact or pipeline to transfer His anointing, power, glory and blessings upon His creation. That is why in a practical sense, just by shaking hands, with people, the anointing is imparted. Just by hugs and holding of hands, the anointing is transferred.Just by coming into contact with an anointed man of God through hugging, the anointing is transferred. This is to tell you that a hand has great significance as a point of impartation in the spirit realm. Prophetically speaking, in this critical end time season which marks the last wave of signs and wonders, during meetings and gatherings as you greet people customarily through shaking hands in the streets, offices or public arena, people fall under the power of God as the anointing is transferred into them. Many business meetings shall be turned into ministerial sessions as the Holy Spirit intensively manifest Himself in an unprecedented wave. Family gatherings shall be turned into prayer meetings, study groups into power groups, dates into divine appointments, cruises into crusades as this uncommon wave of the anointing invades the public arena and other territories which were previously known to be out of bounds where the anointing is concerned. Remember that you are a conveyor of eternal verities and a dispenser of the transcendent life on Christ. As a custodian of God's anointing in this season, while you meet people at the malls, shopping centres, exhibition zones, as you greet, hug and shake hands with people, the anointing shall be imparted and blessings of God transferred. This is because we are the stewards of the anointing hence, we have been granted a heavenly right to channel the anointing in whatever direction we deem necessarily through hand shaking. In a ministerial content, you can command the sick to stand in a queue and shake their hands and impart the healing anointing.

Practical demonstration

I'm reminded of the day that God used me to demonstrate the handshaking anointing at the workplace. Early in the morning as we gathered for our daily meeting session, I felt a prompting in my spirit, hence I burst forth into the following decrees:

I'm a custodian of God's power; I carry God everywhere I go. I carry Him in my heart, in my mouth, in my legs and in my hands. My hands are not my hands but God's hands hence, when I shake people's hands, it is God actually shaking them; my voice is not my voice but God speaking through me, hence when I speak, the word in my mouth is actually God talking. My hands are a symbol of God's power and an instrument to propagate God's glory to the furthest extremes of the world. Therefore, as I shake hands, hug and greet people, the anointing is transferred and blessings are transacted.

As soon as I finished confessing these words, I was so charged in my spirit such that when I took a prophetic step and stretched out my hand to greet one of my colleagues, as my hand came into contact with his, he fell under the power. As I reached out to shake the next person, him too fell under the power. As everybody was perplexed as to what manner of greeting sends people on the floor, I decided to stop, hence I reached out to a lady nearby and hugged her. Strikingly, she too received a double dose of the anointing such that she fell under the power with a loud cry. Being overwhelmed by this spectacular divine experience and being conscious of my code of conduct at the work place, especially the fact that I was now beginning to draw the attention of everybody, I decided to stand at a distance from the people but strikingly, just by saying *"Hie"* to people at a distance, the anointing was transferred to them such that they fell under the power. Just by accidentally waving my hands to someone at a distance, the power of God touched them. When people noticed that the anointing was being transferred as I hugged, and greeted people, they came in large numbers to make a withdrawal and they got blessed. That morning, what was meant to be a business meeting, was actually turned into a Holy Ghost meeting, glory to God! From that day onwards, I officially became an ATM of God's power at the workplace where everybody could freely make a withdrawal.

38. VOICE OR VOCAL ANOINTING

"Demonstrating the Anointing through vocal codes"

This is a kind of anointing that is transferred through speech or voice or sound. It is transferred through vocal codes and is released when you speak or say something. Just by greeting people, the anointing is transferred. At the work place, as you greet your boss, colleagues, the anointing is imparted. This is expressed through voice projection manifested through talking, shouting, and singing, laughing and screaming. In this end time season, as worshipers sing, people shall fall under the power and be healed without any laying of hands. The Walls of Jericho fell down at the sound of people's voices. That is the operation of the vocal anointing. The Bible records an interesting incident whereby the Syrian army heard the footsteps of the four lepers as if they were a thunder of chariots and they all ran away. In other words, the lepers were catapulted to that dimension of the anointing such that their footsteps were heard in the natural realm as the sound of thunder in the spirit realm. This is to tell you that any sound in the natural realm, no matter how small, can be amplified under the anointing such that a whisper can sound like a roar. Remember that when Jesus spoke to Paul on the road to Damascus that his companions had different versions and interpretations of the same divine experience. Others said it roared while others said it thundered, yet Jesus gave Paul such a simple instruction. This tells me that He didn't shout at all. The whisper of His voice in the spirit was heard as a thunder or roar in the natural realm.

CHAPTER FIVE

DEMONSTRATING THE FLOW OF THE ANOINTING UPON OBJECTS

The sacred use of oil was for anointing things or persons in consecrating them to God, as when Jacob anointed the pillar which he had used as a stone for resting his head (Genesis 28:18). This to tell you that the

anointing can rest on anything – whether living or non-living objects such as people, clothes, buildings, air, walls, floor, trees and atmosphere. It is of paramount significance that I emphasise here that you should never play with the anointing. Make sure that as you demonstrate it in various ways, in the process people should healed, delivered, saved and have their faith strengthened in God. Don't just be excited that you are able to demonstrate the anointing or make people fall under the power. While you enjoy the benefits of being anointed, make sure that it benefits humanity in the extreme quarters of the world.

39. DEMONSTRATING THE FLOW OF THE ANOINTING

USING MIKES

During a ministerial session, I touched the mike to transmit the anointing onto it. I then randomly selected seven people in the congregation who had coughing problems and told them to prepare themselves spiritually by asking for forgiveness and for grace. Each of them went to the mike and hold it. They reacted as if they were experiencing some electric shock and were slain in the Spirit. When they got up, they found their coughs gone. Later, many others who wanted healing for their coughs too lined up, touched the mike, and were healed in a similar fashion.

I then commented, The point is this: the healing is done by the anointing and not by the human vessel. The anointing can be on the human vessel and it can be on any material thing. If you want to receive such an anointing from God, you must prepare yourself. God is faithful and He will bless you accordingly. Some ways of transmitting this kind of anointing have been declared in the Word. For example, the woman with the issue of blood had the wisdom to touch the hem of Jesus' garment and was healed. She touched the source of power.

40. DEMONSTRATING THE FLOW OF THE ANOINTING USING A RED CARPET

Do you know that as part of a practical demonstration of the anointing, you can walk on the street and release the anointing and then ask people to walk in the same footsteps or street you have walked and the anointing will begin to hit them and they will fall under the power? Imagine if you were to release this anointing on streets where millions of people walk every day. Imagine the kind of mass healing and deliverance this kind of anointing can breed. The Bible makes it clear that whatsoever land we shall set our foot on is blessed (Joshua 1:3) and one of the manifestations of God's blessings is through the anointing. This follows that as I walk in the streets or whichever territory I step on, I can literally transfer the anointing of God in those places such that if they were not productive before, suddenly fruitfulness comes. The anointing is an expression of God's blessings towards man. Whenever God wants to bless His people, He communicates His grace or blessings through the anointing.

I stood on a carpet for a while and then walked away. I then asked three ladies to stand on the same carpet, one by one, and as they stood, they manifested violently and the demons left them. I then stood again on the same mat and increased the anointing on the carpet. I declared. *"This anointing on this mat will make you paralyzed like a statue."* I then called two men and one woman to stand on the carpet. As each one of them stood on the carpet, they suddenly froze and became like statues. They lifted them one by one like they were carrying statues and laid them on the floor. When I clapped my hands, they came out of their frozen state and became normal. After that, they were trembling and crying because of the fear that they may not come out of the frozen state.

I then stood on the pulpit and gave an instruction to the congregation that I had transferred the anointing on the floor or ground and as soon as I declared that, everyone who was standing on his feet fell under the power.

92

This is to tell you that every ground on which we stride our feet can actually be a good conductor of the anointing of God.

41. DEMONSTRATING THE FLOW OF THE ANOINTING USING A TABLE OR A CHAIR

It is worth mentioning the fact that a table or a chair in itself does not have power because it is an inanimate object. However, God's ability can be imparted upon the chair such that it is enabled to do what God can do. Are you not surprised that a chair can acquire the same divine attributes of God and thus operate with Heavenly efficiency. Are you not amazed that when Jesus was told to instruct His disciples to keep quiet as they shouted during His triumphal entry in Jerusalem, He actually responded by *saying if they keep quiet, these very stones will cry out*? This means that it was possible for God to impart His anointing on stones so that they would praise Jesus just like what human beings would have done. This is to tell you that inanimate objects can perform better than human beings when they are anointed.

Acting on this revelation, I took a table placed it at the front of the church and then transferred the anointing by simply touching it. I then randomly called a group of people from the congregation who needed deliverance from demonic attacks, healing and breakthrough to come and touch the table at once. As their hands came into contact with it, they all flung backwards before they fell under the power. Instantly demons went out of them. Those who were sick were healed band those who needed a breakthrough in divergent spheres of life received them. Taking this demonstration further, I asked a group of 7 people to come and touch the same desk and this time, instead of them falling under the power, they were stuck or glued onto the table. In other words, they were arrested by the anointing of God. This type of the anointing will be increasingly demonstrated to arrest thieves who would want to steal property belonging to children of God.

On a different note, I then touched a chair and transferred the anointing. I then asked one of the sisters in the church who had a womb problem to come and sit on the chair. The instant she sat on the chair, she was so stuck and glued to it such that she couldn't move. I then commanded the church to loose her and let her go, in the same way Jesus commanded the grave clothes to loose Lazarus and let him go. At the sound of my voice, she instantly stood up and all her womb complications and pain had left her.

42. DEMONSTRATING THE FLOW OF THE ANOINTING USING A WALL

Did you know that any object in the natural realm can be used as a vehicle to transmit the anointing of God? A wall made of brick and mortar is a bad conductor of electricity. It can't even allow any flow of electrons but when it comes into contact with the anointing, it can actually heal the sick and drive out demons from people who happen to touch it. As a minister, you can literally conduct a deliverance through a wall and just step aside and watch the demons being roasted by the fire imparted on the wall. John G. Lake in one of his books, talks about how one African preacher sat on a rock to pray and afterwards got many people healed by making them sit on the same rock to receive the anointing. Both the wall and the rock are bad conductors of the power of God but once they come into contact with the anointing, they are able to do what any anointed minister would do under the anointing. Although these inanimate objects cannot preach, yet they have the ability to demonstrate the anointing in a similar fashion in which a believer would demonstrate it.

Inspired by this revelation, in a service, I touched the part of the front wall where I was ministering and transferred the anointing. I then declared that *anyone who will come into contact with this part of the wall will receive a touch from God.* I then called all those who needed to receive the Holy Spirit, the anointing or touch from God to come and receive the anointing by touching the wall. They came in masses and the instant their hands came into contact with the wall, they fell under the power and received the Holy Ghost with the evidence of speaking in other tongues and some instantly burst forth into prophetic utterances, glory to God!

One of these days I'm looking forward to demonstrating the anointing of the wall but literally walking through the wall. I'm looking for an opportunity when the anointing is present so that I can demonstrate God's ability by actually passing through a wall in the same way Jesus entered the house through the wall, where His disciples gathered after His resurrection. For someone who is saying, but Jesus' body was now glorified, what about ours? Have you not read how our bodies have been vitalised by the indwelling of the Holy Spirit? Through the indwelling presence of the Holy Spirit, our bodies can actually take on a supernatural quality that enables them to either walk in the air or pass through a wall.

CHAPTER SIX

DEMONSTRATING THE FLOW OF THE ANOINTING USING CLOTHES

43. DEMONSTRATING THE FLOW OF THE ANOINTING USING A JACKET

The Bible records thrilling examples of how the anointing of God's spirit was demonstrated using clothes. When Elijah was caught up by chariots of fire, his sash which had absorbed greater volumes of the anointing throughout his entire life, fell upon Elisha, who grabbed it and used it to cast River Jordan and divined its waters. There are other instances whereby aprons and handkerchiefs were taken from the body of Paul and then laid on the sick and the demon possessed such that they were healed and evil spirits left them. In fact, a jacket represent the anointing in the spirit realm and casting it upon the crowd is a way of casting the real tangible substance of the anointing upon the masses. I'm reminded of Jacob's garment of many colours which caused him to be hated by his brothers. Although this was just a simple jacket, in the realm of the spirit, it represented authority and a greater anointing. The element of different colours represented the different giftings and graces which comes with authority and power. During ministerial sessions, at times, I find myself in the position of Joseph, having to demonstrate a greater anointing in the light of envy from my fellow brothers in Christ across the globe.

Basing my unwavering faith upon these revelations, during an anointing service, I commanded the crowd to be ready to receive a greater dimension of the anointing. I then took off my jacket which had been absorbing the anointing and threw it on the crowd. A spectacular display of power was witnessed as the whole congregation, totalling thousands of people fell under the power. In the same meeting, I demonstrated how the anointing was transferred from the hem of Jesus's garment into the woman with a flow of blood when she touched him. Acting on this revelation, I asked those who were sick in their bodies to come and touch just the hem of my jacket and to my surprise, as they touched, they were instantly healed, glory to Jesus! This is to tell you that under the anointing, you can actually demonstrate any miracle which is chronicled in the pages of the Bible.

44. DEMONSTRATING THE FLOW OF THE ANOINTING USING A HAND BAG

Who would have ever known that a handbag can actually be used to demonstrate the anointing? It's amazing how under the anointing, we are enabled to change the function of an object into something else of which it was not originally intended. I asked for a hand bag from one of the sisters who was sitting at the front of the congregation and then transferred the anointing by touching it. then called two people on stage. I commanded one lady to take the bag and walk across the aisle as if she is walking alone in the street. I also commanded the young man to pretend as if he is a thief and attempt to take the bag away from the woman by force. As the lady took the bag and walked by as per my instruction, the young man jumped on her in an attempt to grab the bag. Instantly, what appeared to be an arrow of power shot through him and flew him up before he could land on the floor with a thud. Everyone in the congregation was amazed at the alacrity by which the young man was flung into the air. He lay there motionless until I prayed for him to be restored. This was just a divine experiment. Imagine what would have happened to him if he were a real thief.

In the end times, the Lord will release a special anointing for protection over His chosen vessels. People may come in numbers to attack His chosen vessels, but when they draw near to them, they will be frozen on the spot. Their friends and relatives would have to carry them away in that state as if they are carrying statues. It would be a matter of weeks or days before they die. The only person who would be able to release them from their frozen state would be the chosen vessels whom they tried to attack. If the believer comes and prays over them, they would be healed, but if he chooses not to come, these people would perish.

45. DEMONSTRATING THE FLOW OF THE ANOINTING USING A SHOE

It is worth exploring the truth that not only can we demonstrate the anointing using our hands but we can use our feet too. In the spirit realm, the feet represent mobility and strength. Hence, there is a type of anointing which can be demonstrated through the use of a shoe. I During a service under the unction, I called out all those who had problems with their feet or legs to come and receive their healing. I then gently stepped on their feet and transferred the anointing and instantly they received their healing. I also stood on stage and asked those who were sick to come and touch my shoes and the anointing was transferred from my spirit into my body and from my body into my shoe and from the shoe into the masses and they were flung backwards as they came into contact with the anointing.

Taking this demonstration to a higher level, I walked across the stage and in the process transferring the anointing onto the ground. I then asked those who experience demonic attacks to come and walk where I have walked and stamp their feet on the same ground where I had walked and as they did, they fell under the power and the demons cried out and instantly left their bodies. This is to tell you that even the ground can conduct the anointing of God. That is why any sick person who happen to enter into your yard should be healed instantly because of the anointing that is flowing on the floor of your yard. You can use your royal prerogative as a son of God to demarcate certain territories and declare them as Holy Ground, such that anybody who happen to tread on them, receives the power of God.

46. DEMONSTRATING THE FLOW OF THE ANOINTING USING A HANDKERCHIEF

The Bible records a spectacular incident whereby handkerchiefs were taken from the body of Paul and laid on the sick such that they were healed. A handkerchief makes it easy for the power of God to be transferred to places such as the hospitals to heal the sick and also to the mortuaries, to raise the dead. Did you know that you can actually transfer the resurrection anointing on a handkerchief and then take it and lay it on a dead person and he will rise up? In this end time season, not only will handkerchiefs be used to heal the sick but they shall also be used to raise the dead as humanity is catapulted into the realm of resurrection power. We have just entered into a season whereby raising the dead is increasingly becoming a widespread phenomenon across the Body of Christ. This shall accentuate an avenue for such demonstrations to be staged. Acting on this revelation, I walked in the footsteps of Paul, the apostle, took out a handkerchief from my pocket and then called out two groups of people, first all those with any type of sickness to come and receive their healing and secondly those who were demon posed or afflicted by demons through nightmares to come and receive their deliverance. As the handkerchief came into contact with them, they were instantly healed and those with demons they writhed and demons left them without struggle, glory to God!

CHAPTER SEVEN

PRACTICAL DEMONSTRATION OF THE MINISTERIAL ANOINTING

It is an anointing given to a man for the work of ministry. The second level of anointing is when God anoints the believer for a particular ministry that God has called him or her to do. Everyone in the Body of Christ is called to be in ministry. There is to be no competition or comparisons among believers, as each of us is given a unique assignment from the Master (Jesus) to fulfil. Not all are called to clergy ministry, but all are called to fulfil a specific ministry assignment that God has given each of us to do. The believer does not have to go in their own strength to minister, but goes in the Name of the Lord and is endued with the power and anointing of the Holy Spirit to carry out their particular ministry assignment. God's anointing for ministry equips us with the skill, ability, wisdom and favour to function in their area of ministry. God's anointing for ministry will bring about fruitfulness.

The most important thing about the ministerial anointing is that it is so diversified. An individual can flow in different types of anointing at one time. At different times, you can flow in some, then in one, and then sometimes in none and then in three types of anointing again. When you look at the whole picture, you see a colourful flow of the Holy Spirit.

God ordains all the five-fold ministries to spearhead and lead the revival and the move of God. When you could release the five-fold ministry, you release the revival of God. The five-fold offices train and build the body for the church ministry. As we look at the book of Acts, we realize that when the church first started it was a powerful church. There was the apostolic ministry but it was even more powerful when the prophets start coming out from them. By Acts 8, you read about evangelists coming out from them. By Acts 11 you read about prophets coming out from them. The church

98

was even more powerful. Every time you have all the five-fold offices functioning, the church is at its peak. However, every time you begin to lose one or two of those offices functioning, there is a low coming in. If ever the churches reach a point where all five were not functioning or one office is functioning, it is just a shadow of a revival. So, it would be sad in the body of Christ if all you have were just the office of pastor. It would be sad in the body of Christ if all you have were just prophets. So, we have to know that we need all of them. We need prophets in the church. We need evangelists in the church. We need pastors and teachers in the church. We need apostles in the church. We need all five-fold offices to function. If the body of Christ lacks any one of them they will not see the full revival that God wants us to have.

Our Lord Jesus Christ functioned in all five offices when He was on this earth. He was an apostle (Hebrews 3:1); He was a prophet (Acts 3:22-26); He was an evangelist (Mark 1:14); He was a pastor, which is the same word as shepherd (John 10:11); He was a teacher (Mark 4:1-2) as recognised by Nicodemus (John 3:2). So, Jesus Christ stood in all the five ministerial anointing, the fivefold office the office of an apostle, the office of a prophet, the office of an evangelist, the office of a pastor and the office of a teacher. Jesus stood in each of the five-fold office. And what happened is in the book of Ephesians 4:8. Therefore He says; *"When He ascended on high, He led captivity captive, and gave gifts to men."* (Now this, *"He ascended"* – what does it mean but that He also first descended into the lower parts of the earth? He who descended is also the One who ascended far above all the heavens, that He might fill all things.) *And He Himself gave some to be apostles, some prophets, come evangelists, and some pastors and teachers. For the equipping of the saints for the work of ministry, for the edifying of the body of Christ.*

So, when Jesus Christ ascended, He delegated the offices that He stood in and poured the anointing to somebody else. Remember that God from time to time may change vessel or vessels may complete their work but the offices will continue. Like when Elijah completed his work and went off, Elisha stood in his place. Whenever a man of God completes his work and goes home to be with God, his office is actually vacant for the taking. The five-fold ministries are for all generations from the time the church started until Jesus comes again since it's for the perfecting of the church Notice the same trend in the Old Testament. God ordains only three offices in the Old Testament. They are the prophets, priests and kings. Sometimes the office is left vacant. Why? It's because the men whom God called in that generation were not obedient. So, a particular office may lack a man in that particular generation. Sometimes God may appoint one man to stand in one or two or three offices so that he could minister fully to that generation. Moses had a peculiar kind of anointing. Moses stood in three offices. Moses was a prophet and Moses was a judge and that's carries a kingly anointing though not in its full extent yet. So, Moses functioned in all three and there were times when he had to balance between all three offices. If you watch Kenneth Hagin's ministry, he functioned less in certain types of anointing and he concentrates more on just the teaching anointing. But in the early days of his ministry he functioned more in the prophetic than in the teaching. So how do we co-relate the five-fold ministry? We recognize that as far as in the area of the church is concerned the apostolic and the pastoral office have a greater authority. But in the area of the Word of God and doctrine the teacher has a greater authority. In the area of reaching out to the world, the evangelist has a greater authority. In the area of direction and the future the prophet has the greatest authority. When God sends you out, it's not so much you can teach as to what God wants the people to hear His voice at that hour.

47. THE PROPHETIC ANOINTING

When it comes to the prophetic anointing there are similarities involved but they are also different realms. That is No. 1 you must perceive and launch into the area of training your spiritual eyes. See in the olden days, a prophet is also called a seer. In Samuel's time you notice the prophets are called seers. Because they are people accustomed to seeing visions and revelations. Some people seem to be born with that slant towards visions and dreams. Others seem to be required to develop it. But whatever it is, the slant or the special gifting or talent that God has for you still needs development. You could be the most gifted, talented musician but if you don't go for training I doubt that you could ever develop your gifts. So the gift is one thing and the training is another. We need to understand the operation of each so that it may be that when God wanted us to grow into that area when you understand it you could be trained into that.

There are certain essentials of prophetic anointing. In the prophetic anointing, you would need what we call an atmosphere. You need a certain atmosphere where the spirits of people are in contact with God before you could move into that prophetic gift of God. For example, look at 2 Kings 3:15 *"But now bring me a musician." Then it happened, when the musician played, that the hand of the Lord came upon him.* Elisha was asked to prophesy. He was asked to bring the word of the Lord. He stood in the office of a prophet. Even though he stood in the office of a prophet, he cannot do the ministry of a prophet unless his spirit permits him. But he could create the atmosphere where if the spirit willed, the spirit would do so. Of all things he asked for music. The first part of moving deep in prophetic anointing is usually a musical atmosphere or worshipful reverence. The more you could have that in your life, the more you could develop it. If we understand the need for a musical atmosphere to facilitate the prophetic anointing, we would know how to receive a prophet as a prophet and if you understand how a prophetic office operates even if you don't operate it, you could know how to tap on that.

The other key element is Sensitivity. Hagin is also affected to a certain extent when he function in the office of a prophet. In his book, he said there are times the prophet mantle would fall upon him then the worship Leader changes the song or goes into something else and he said the anointing lifted off him like a bird and he has no more prophetic mantle on him. He is a prophet but the anointing is not there to function. So, if we don't understand how the prophet anointing operates we will also in a sense hinder it. So, we have to understand these things to tap on the anointing of God in that realm. If you notice in Israel there were three types of anointing possible in the Old Testament. In the new, there are much more, we have the five-fold, ministry of believers and many types of anointing. But in the Old, there were three main key ministries, the *prophet*, the *priest* and the *king*. Notice that the key point in Israel when it was at its peak was when all the three-fold anointing was functioning. In Samuel's time, he was the one who started the *School of the Prophets*. You see, the anointing can be taught. Samuel must have imparted it but at the time Elisha came to the scene he was with the sons of the prophets. That was the third generation down the line. So, the anointing could be imparted if there is proper training.

It is evident that before a prophetic anointing can function, you need an atmosphere of worship and a correct kind of music to function in. Samuel knew the key and he trained his group of prophets in I Samuel 10:5

After that you shall come to the hill of God where the Philistine garrison is. And it will happen, when you have come there to the city, that you will meet a group of prophets coming down from the high place with a stringed instrument, a tambourine, a flute and a harp before them, and they will be prophesying. Then the Spirit of the Lord will come upon you and you will prophesy with them and be turned into another man.

Notice there was an atmosphere of music. What were the prophets doing? Tongues have not been manifested yet. It's a New Testament dispensation. You see all the gifts of the Spirit manifest except the gift of tongues, which was reserved for the New Testament dispensation. But tongues were not manifested in the Old Testament. So what were they doing? They were prophesying with their understanding with music. Can you imagine being in the atmosphere somebody is saying, *"The Lord is good"*. And they were doing it under a tree. And it's so easy to move into the prophetic anointing. That even when someone was not called to be a prophet like Saul got into contact with them and the Spirit came upon him he started prophesying. It was an atmosphere with that situation. You notice that if you remove music out of some of the movies today, you remove the excitement. It's the music that gets your heart beating fast. It's the music that vibrates your heart.

Now, in the spiritual realm music has an influence too. Remember we mentioned that God does to us has to be through our spirit, soul and physical body. If your mind is not in state of rest where it should be in God, you can never operate in the gift. There has to be a certain state of mind that you are in before you could operate it. So a certain atmosphere must be present. I reckon that if I could have the time to spend about 8 hours with God every day and do nothing, just live like a man of God on a hill somewhere and just have prayer and intercession all around. And you got no administrative work to do, no shopping to do and nothing else to do but just to be with God. I would reckon every time I walk out I would be able to see things in people's life everywhere I go. Why? It's because your state of mind and the atmosphere you are filling yourself with enhances your receptivity to the spirit world.

There are times when you have an atmosphere and you are easily yielded to God, and for those times music, seems crucial. In a prophetic anointing, music in fact is crucial to the function of the whole anointing. Let me show more from I Chronicles 25:1:

> *Moreover David and the captains of the army separated for the service some of the sons of Asaph, of Heman, and of Jeduthun, who should prophesy with harps, stringed instruments, and cymbals. And the number of the skilled men performing that service was: Of the sons of Asaph: Zaccur, Joseph, Nethaniah, and Asharelah, the sons of Asaph were under the direction of Asaph, who prophesied according to the order of the king.*

Notice the word that keep occurring like in verse one who should prophesy with harps, stringed instruments and cymbals. Why does it tie it together with stringed instrument? There is a relationship. In verse 3 under the direction of their father Jeduthun, who prophesied with harp to give thanks and to praise the Lord. Now these are important statements that the bible gives to us. Although David was essentially a king, he tapped into the anointing of prophecy because he was basically a musician and a worshiper of God. We need No. 1 the atmosphere that is created for that prophetic anointing to begin operation. If you provide the right atmosphere where people are called to the ministry of prophets, it will stir that gift and it will raise it forth. Elisha said bring me a minstrel. He moved into the prophetic world. If you want to go into the prophetic realm, go into psalms and songs onto the Lord. Then you move from that psalm into the prophetic realm. In that way, you could develop and train your prophetic gift of God. So No. 1 is the atmosphere.

Secondly, you need Prophetic training, which encompasses the training of your imagination. Remember I said that a prophet is normally called a seer. Kenneth Hagin mentioned in his book, *"The Ministry of a Prophet,"* that for a prophet to stand in the office of a prophet you need two revelations gifts and the gift of prophecy. Revelation gifts have a lot to do with your spiritual senses of sight. And your spiritual sense of sight is linked to your imagination. It is therefore imperative that you keep your vision pure. There are three types of visions. An open vision, close vision and spiritual vision. An open vision is where you can see the natural world and the spiritual world at the same time. A closed vision is where you can see only the spiritual world and none of the physical world. Usually it's in a state of trance. Like Peter was on the rooftop, he fell into a trance and he saw a vision of unclean animals. A spiritual vision, also known as an *inner vision*, is what you see with the inner eyes of your spirit, which is reflected upon the canvas of your imagination. For that reason, people called to be prophets have to be even more careful about watching T.V. or movies since they depend so much on their spiritual sight. So, they are to keep their imagination pure before God so that there won't be any subliminal effect. For example, if you have been watching too much T.V. or movies, then when you come to move in the spirit, the moment you close your eyes you see the echo of what you have seen. Your natural eyes cast the shadow of their images on the screen of your mind and are locked onto your imagination. It's easier to paint a painting on a clean canvas than on a dirty one. Now, every one of us has spiritual eyes. But some of our spiritual eyes are a little bit short sighted. When you close your eyes to see the spiritual world, you see it blurry. The problem is that there are no special glasses for that. The only treatment you have is God's word. Learn to depend on your other senses. That's when I began to tune my spiritual eyes also as they were out of frequency. And I also tuned my hearing. For example sometimes before a meeting I pray and hang loose with the Lord. And I could see some of the things that will take place. Sometimes I could see exactly where people will be sitting. I could see the type of sickness that God wants to heal. What you are doing is in your spirit you have moved into the future. And our spirit can also move into geographical distances. I train my spirit and my mind to the extent that if I so desire I could put my spirit and mind in any place I want. It is not astral traveling. It's relating to the Holy Spirit who gives a revelation like Paul telling the Colossians, *"I behold your order."* To the Corinthians, he says,

"When you put this person aside and pronounce your excommunication and judgment on this guy, my spirit was with yours."

The other key factor is renewal of mind. Whenever you minister to people in the area of prophesying, you see something. If your mind is not so renewed, some of those things you see are distractions. Some of those things we see are from the enemy if we have seen them before in our life. That is why before you move into the anointing you have to be absolutely sure and know within yourself that there is no sin that is not confessed in your life. We are not saying you must be perfect. You don't need to be perfect to move into the anointing but you need to be under the blood. The other element is Sensitivity to what you see in spirit. So, all these are important for us to know that we have to train our inner eyes of our spirit. And in any service that you worship the Lord sometimes gives you to see pictures. A lot of Christians are ignoring them. I know because when God started showing me what His voice is like it was so easy. I told God that I have been ignoring it all the time. He has been speaking but I have been ignoring His voice. I didn't know that some of them sound like my own thoughts. Some of our thoughts come from God, some from the devil and some from our own self. But the thing is that we are missing some of the thoughts that are coming from God through our spirit being.

The other factor is Consecration. Sometimes people think just because they got tickets to fly to another place and teach the word, they have become the five-fold ministry. No. That is not evangelist, that's a tourist. Those who desire to move into God's anointing, you have no choice but to consecrate yourself. Paul Cain would spend hours in his hotel room. He would not speak to anybody. Sometimes he just shows himself for a while, takes a small bite and get back to his room. Then his team members would blind-fold him. Now he does not require that but his concentration would be greater if he does that. In the early days even seeing people can distract what he is seeing in the spirit. So he will blind fold himself and he will go to the meeting. Then he would take out his blindfold and start calling people whom he had seen in the spirit. Why, so that there will be no hindrance in what he is seeing in the eyes of his understanding. Of course a person must choose to open himself in the spirit.

The other factor is the Degree of openness to prophetic. You could sense whether people are opened or not to the Lord's ministry. If the people are closed up to the ministry, the Lord will not violate His free choice. The only possible way is by what I call a supernatural act of which is very rare. The Lord will not reveal a thing about a person's life that doesn't open himself. When you minister to every person like right now as I am speaking to you there is virtually nothing to see in the spiritual realm. But as I open my spirit after God and if I am ministering in the area of prophecy, I begin to see things in the spirit. The last area, which we have already operated in, is to hear the interpretation of the vision we saw. Now hearing is important because if you don't hear correctly your application is wrong. And your hearing is fine-tuned by your knowledge of the word. The background in the word of God is going to affect your ability to apply what you see. Some people see something in the spirit but they cannot interpret the meaning, so therefore they cannot apply it. And it doesn't benefit at all. The background that we have in the knowledge of the word is going to help us and apply in our lives in that area.

Practical demonstration

In the end times, there will be an accelerated mountain of anointing on chosen vessels. God will take the anointing on these chosen vessels and transmit it to their co-workers during the service. They will then multiply the work all over the place during the service. Under the anointing of the Holy Spirit, I moved in the prophetic instruction and commanded everybody to receive the prophetic anointing and many started prophesying on the spot. Some started making prophetic utterances, prophetic gestures and other diverse manifestations.

48. THE HEALING ANOINTING

When operating or moving in the healing anointing there are three keys that are paramount. *No.1 is the manifestation. No.2 is understanding the manifestation. No.3 channelling the manifestation.* There are two main dimensions in the healing anointing and these are *healing by the anointing* and *healing by faith*. Most Christians have not understood aspects of the healing anointing. Sometimes my heart cries when I see people trying to minister healing by faith when the healing anointing is not there. Sometimes wheelchair bound people try to rise up to their feet and they fall back again because there was no healing anointing. They were just trying to walk by faith. But the healing anointing and walking by faith are different operations from each other. Trying to get healing by faith and getting it by the anointing are two different ways. There are two ways you can get healing from God. One is by personal faith and confessing the word. The other is by the healing anointing. Sometimes it is God who decides which method He uses to release healing to you. If I don't sense the healing anointing to heal a person that way, I would encourage that person to go on the word and receive healing through exercising faith in the word. Regardless of which methods God uses, it is always His will to heal. It is always God's will to heal. Sometimes in services, we see a river of life flowing out that makes the lame to walk and the blind to see. However, at meetings where the healing anointing is not present, after the meeting the lame go home still lame and the blind still blind. There is the presence of something somewhere that we need to grapple with. That is called the *healing anointing*.

To substantiate this divine truth with reference to scriptural evidence, let's consider what the narrative in Mark 5:25 says:

> *Now, a certain woman had a flow of blood for twelve years, and had suffered many things from many physicians. She had spent all that she had and was no better, but rather grew worse. When she heard about Jesus she came behind Him in the crowd and touched His garment. For she said, "If only I may touch His clothes, I shall be made well." Immediately the fountain of her blood was dried up, and she felt (I want to emphasize that and she felt) in her body that she was healed of the affliction.*

That's the *healing anointing* demonstrated here. Notice the word, *"Jesus immediately"*. It means it didn't take long as it was immediately. Jesus didn't take ten sentences of prayer. It doesn't mean that the longer you pray the stronger you get. And Jesus, immediately knowing in Himself that power had gone out of Him, turned around in the crowd and said, *"Who touched Me?"* Jesus Christ felt a power flowing out from Him. We are not talking about getting healing by faith. We are talking about getting healing by the *healing anointing*, and when there is a healing anointing, it is very easy to get healing.

But there is a way to tap on the healing anointing. There is a way that the healing anointing flows. We must be sensitive to know when the healing anointing is not present so that we can switch to ministering by faith. The healing anointing is tangible. Tangible means it is touchable. The healing anointing is some force that you can feel and touch. When you minister under the anointing, you better be sure that you know and recognize the anointing when it comes. If you do not sense the anointing, then you cannot minister by the anointing. You have to minister by faith. I make sure I do not minister under the anointing unless I sense the anointing. If I don't sense it, I would get twenty people to keep worshiping until the anointing comes. But the anointing is tangible. It is touchable. You can feel it. The woman felt it when it flowed into her. Jesus felt it when it flowed out from Him. There is a certain atmosphere about the anointing. Notice that the woman had exercised her faith. Earlier on she said, " *If I touch His garments, I shall be made well. She had gone through the normal process of faith.* "Firstly, she had heard about Jesus. She had heard all about the miracles of Jesus. And she had received a certain measure of faith. When she heard about the miracles of Jesus, she started believing. When she believed, she said, *"Oh, I wish I could see Him or touch Him. I believe all those miracles that happened."* She had met the blind, the lepers and the lame people who were healed. The testimonies were coming back to her. Notice people need to hear first. And before they hear somebody must speak. If there were no speakers, there would be no hearers. That is why if God has done something in your life you need to share with others to glorify God and bolster the faith of others. When you share your testimony, others are encouraged to have faith in God. Faith comes by hearing and if no one speaks, there is no hearing.

Confessing by faith and sharing your testimony are different from each other. Testimony is sharing your story when you have already been healed and everybody can see you are healed. Confessing by faith is saying the same thing as the word, *"I believe I receive,"* even before the healing is manifested. That's a confession. But testimony is different. When God had done something in your life, you need to go and share. And when you share God's wonderful work in you, people's faith is built up. The woman heard the word. Then she started confessing her faith and I don't know how often. Another person comes and shares with her another testimony and she said, *"I wish I could be there. If I could only touch the hem of His garment."* If I were to come behind you and touch your sari, you wouldn't feel anything at all, unless there are nerve endings embedded in your clothing and connected to your nervous system. Unless somebody pulls your sari, then you feel the force pulling you. The woman merely touched; she didn't pull. Yet Jesus felt a spiritual force flowing out of His physical body.

I want you to know that *there is a difference between exercising your faith and tapping on the healing anointing.* See, the woman was constantly confessing her faith and there was no manifestation until she touched Jesus. People don't realize that there is a difference between belief and faith and they tend to mix them up. When they said they believe they thought that that's it. But faith is a tangible force. It has to do with the healing anointing. The faith in question here is not your personal faith. I know some people illustrate by saying you need to have faith in everything. You must have faith in the chair that the chair will hold you up. When the healing anointing flows into you, you don't need somebody next to you to tell you that you are healed. You know that you are healed. When the Spirit of adoption came on you, you know that you are a child of God. The Spirit bears witness with your spirit. When the healing anointing comes on you, you know that you know, that you are healed. Something moved inside you. There is a tangible sensing of God's power. People don't differentiate the two; *the healing anointing* and *exercising of faith*. Sometimes your heart can weep for those people seeking for healing. I mean people who are needy and suffering. Most of them don't want their sicknesses. Sometimes instead of waiting and getting on the healing anointing to flow, we try to minister healing by our belief. What people mean by belief is usually trust. But the healing anointing and the faith of God are different from your faith in God.

The healing anointing works stronger when people are seeking for Jesus and not seeking for healing. But when you are getting people to exercise faith for healing, people need to believe that healing belongs to them. See the healing anointing requires a different type of operation altogether. My heart feels grieved because I see people not flowing with the healing anointing properly. When the healing anointing is present, they do not sense it and attempt to minister healing through confessing the word and exercising their personal faith. No, when the healing anointing is present, you hear the instructions of the Holy Spirit and act accordingly. If you just keep confessing the word when the healing anointing is present, you block the Holy Spirit from speaking to you. That is why I am grieved. That is why the Holy Spirit is grieved and He can lift His anointing up when the leaders do not wait for His instructions.

That's why when the healing anointing has descended on a congregation; I am not too concerned whether anyone in the crowd is born again or not. The *healing anointing* comes as a free gift. Please note these words that when the healing anointing comes it is the gift of God working. A gift is not something you deserve. A gift is something freely given to you. It's a gift of His grace to you. And grace is not something you earn, not because you confess the word many times or you do enough good works. But the gift of God is where God just showers His gift on you. And when it drops on you, you know that you know that you are healed. That's the healing anointing flowing. Do not give any specific command to any person unless the healing anointing has descended on you. However, if there are about twenty wheel chair cases, you may give a general command and the gift of God may operate for three. But the next day the other seven may be touched and healed. See, the gift of God operates differently. In Kathryn Kuhlman's meetings, the most important thing is the presence of the Holy Spirit. Some people may come for the first time and they are not healed. They come again and they are still not healed. They come the third time and they are finally

108

healed. Why? Wouldn't it be foolish if the first time the wheelchair bound person comes and you force the person to stand? If he didn't get healed, he might feel condemned after that. That's the way God's Spirit will work and move. We want to learn how the healing anointing flows so that we can be smooth open channels for the Holy Spirit to move.

I want to share something through my experience on the healing anointing. In Acts 3:2, a certain man lame from his mother's womb was carried, whom they laid daily at the gates of the temple which is called Beautiful, to ask alms from those who enter the temple; And the lame man was there every day. Every day he was worshiping God but there was a time when the healing anointing was flowing. I want you to know that you are to keep holding to your faith and let the sick come because healing is not your business, it is God's business. I want you to be sensitive to the Holy Spirit anointing. When there is a time when the healing anointing flows and you do your part, God does His part. God has never asked you to do the impossible. He is the one who does that but He asked you to do your part. Every day that lame man was there in the temple, he was not healed and nobody put any condemnation on him. If people keep condemning those who are not healed in one service, they might never come again. At a certain time there are some forces at work within a person's life. Sometimes at a certain stage the healing anointing rests on that person. At that stage, healing can take place. I feel sad when I sense that the sick could be healed if the congregation just keep worshiping and praising God and letting the presence of God soak into him or her. Perhaps by the fourth meeting when the worship and expectation of the people has grown high and the Lord is pleased to release His healing anointing, then when the command is given, mighty miracles take place all over the auditorium.

Don't be in a hurry to palm healing off to people. He that believes does not make haste. But one day in the fullness of time, the Holy Spirit releases His healing anointing on the congregation. I like that word in the fullness of time because the Holy Spirit is so gentle. How do we know when a person's heart is right with God? You cannot know fully. See man always looks at the outward whereas God looks at the inward. Only God knows the intricate secrets that go on in a person's heart. Sometime in the fullness of time a person is ready for the healing anointing to come. They don't come accidentally. But there are issues inside a person's life that God is dealing with that you do not see. And sometimes that person reaches the fullness of time and if you are sensitive to the healing anointing you will sense it too. This is something that Peter did that I never understood for the first three years of my ministry. Finally I understood. That lame man, seeing Peter and John about to go into the temple, asked for alms. Somebody said that he asked for arm and he got leg. Verse 4 I never understood before And fixing his eyes on him, with John, Peter said, "*Look at us.*" I never understood why he needed to do that. After all, God calls us to the preaching, teaching and healing business. He never called us to be in the staring business. It is very rude to stare. People don't like you to stare at them. But verse 4 Peter fixing his eyes on him. And the first word he says was not, "*In the name of Jesus Christ, walk.*"

I did ask the Holy Spirit about this years back. Why didn't he just say in the name of Jesus? If he did that he wouldn't have been sensing the healing anointing. What Peter was sensing was the healing anointing. I agree that if it were a matter of healing by exercising of personal faith, then we ought to command healing in the name of Jesus. I have seen cases where leaders try to cast out demons using their personal faith and six hours later, they are still trying to cast them out. They say, "*Come out.*" The demon said, "*No.*" "*Come out.*" "*No.*" They try everything they have learnt from books with little success. But when the anointing comes you just say, "*In Jesus' name.*" and the demon will just go out. There is a difference when the anointing is there. The Holy Spirit says the first words of people are as important as the rest. Remember this man has been in the temple for many days. They had prayer meetings every day. Nowadays you call for prayer meetings after office hours and not many people would come. They have church seven days a week. Some people will say that will take my whole life. But didn't you tell the Lord that He is Lord over your whole life and yet, the next moment He wants to take your whole life you say no. Your whole life has to revolve around Jesus.

In another incident in Acts 14 this is the prayer of the healing anointing. Verse 8 And in Lystra a certain man without strength in his feet was sitting, a cripple from his mother's womb, who had never walked. This man heard Paul speaking. Faith comes by hearing and hearing by the word. We think that its just simple you hear you get it. I tell you there are a lot of hindrances to hearing. I am not talking about hearing physically but hearing spiritually. All of you can be hearing the same message but receive different messages and revelations. Every one of us can hear the same message and come out with different degrees of faith. That is why it is not what we hear but as Jesus said, "*Take heed how you hear.*" Hearing has to do with the attentiveness of your inner man. This man was hearing Paul very intensely. Somehow faith got into him. We would have thought that every sick person who comes when they hear the teaching of the word would receive faith but not all. Only God knows the heart. He does not reveal the heart of man to us all the time but sometimes He may reveal. There are certain things in a person's life that though the word is speaking they never heard it. They heard physically but they never heard it inside. But some people can be in the same meeting, hear the same message, it goes right into them and faith cometh by hearing. So only God knows the heart. That's why we need to be sensitive to God picking up those whom He says has touched Him and He will touch them.

This man in verse 9 heard Paul speaking and Paul was observing him intently. As Paul was preaching in an open-air meeting, his eyes were just fixing on this person. What was he seeing? The same thing that the cripple saw. As I preach and teach, I can see if people are touched by God or not. There is something that you can see when a person has touched and contacted God. As we worship God most of the time we close our eyes but sometimes when I open my eyes, I can see whether people are touched by the worship or not. And God touches those who have touched God. So as Paul was preaching and teaching, he was observing and he saw a lame man observing intently. He saw that the man had faith to be healed. This is not something that you can see with your natural eyes. You need revelation to pick up that. That refers back to Peter in Acts 3 verse 4 he was looking for faith to be healed. It is a spiritual quality. When you move under the healing anointing, it is the gift of healing that God has imparted in a general congregation. That is why worship is important. We need to contact God first. So when you worship God and you contact God, He starts releasing His healing anointing on the congregation and dropping His gift of faith in individuals here and there who have touched Him. Such mustard seeds of God's faith imparted in them enable them to tap on the healing anointing and receive healing. He starts operating and doing interesting things. I know it when the Holy Spirit takes charge. But we need to touch God first before He touches us with that precious mustard seed of faith. So, there are certain things about being in the presence of God. That's why if a person really wants to be healed, he ought to come for every meeting. There is something about touching God and God touching you. So, when Paul was preaching the word, he was sensitive to the Holy Spirit imparting His gift of faith to individuals here and there. One of them was the cripple who received God's faith in him and Paul saw that faith of God in that cripple's eyes. See it's the faith that's imparted. If it is your own faith, it won't do much. But it is God's faith.

How much of God's faith do you need? You don't need a mountain of faith. You don't need a tone of faith. Some people see patients being brought in on stretchers and they feel they need a tone of faith. But they are thinking of their personal faith. When the healing anointing descends on a meeting, just a mustard seed of God's faith imparted to you is enough to release the healing to the people. I tell you, if you have a tone of faith,

111

you won't be on this planet earth. You would be too powerful and you may even explode the whole world. The seed of God is a powerful substance. When the seed of God comes into you, something happens. Jesus said in Matthew 17 if you have faith like a grain of mustard seed. You know how small a mustard seed is. Jesus was using one of the smallest seeds known to man. If you have faith like a mustard seed, just one dot is enough to move mountains. How much more when you have a ton of faith, which is equivalent to one billion trillion of mustard seeds. That is why I say you have to be very sensitive to the Holy Spirit and hear Him carefully to reveal who among the crowd has received that seed of the faith of God. That mustard seed is important. It drops into a person's heart in the intricate labyrinths of the inner soul. One mustard seed faith can move a mountain. It is like one little grain against Goliath. By the time you have a ton of faith I say it will explode mountain ranges all over the world and you will not have enough mountains to move. A mustard seed of faith is already so power packed. One tiny drop of mustard faith in you and instantly you will be healed.

But then you must know when the healing anointing is imparted. God does everything by faith. You see faith is alive with the life of God. See it is a substance in (Hebrews 11:1). So the healing anointing when it moves it imparts the life of God. And the life of God is a life force. It's the faith of God imparted. When the life and healing of God is imparted to people, they feel a refreshing, a bubbling and stirring inside them. That's a manifestation. It's a tangible mustard seed faith imparted. And Paul; in Act 14 when he was preaching he saw that man lying there that he had faith through the perception of the Spirit. When that happen you can give a command. I am not talking about giving command when you are being half filled with the Spirit. You know what I mean by being half filled. It is still better than none but still, it is too small a measure to release the grace of God or the favour of God or see the gifts of God imparted. I am not talking about getting healed by personal faith. I am talking about being so filled with the Spirit that your spirit man can easily receive the gift of healing, the gift of working of miracles and the gift of faith when the healing anointing descends. These are the power gifts. The gifts of God are imparted like an influx. At the same time that the Holy Spirit releases the healing anointing, He also releases the mustard seed of the faith of God in individuals here and there to enable them to tap on the healing anointing and receive healing. Thus, when the Spirit-filled minister gives the command and the mustard seed faith-filled individuals hear the command, an explosion of healing occurs in the latter. That mustard seed faith will move a mountain of years of paralysis. God gets the glory for both releasing the healing anointing and the mustard seeds of the faith of God. God does everything. `We wait for His manifestation and while waiting we worship Him. I am talking about the healing anointing and not about exercising personal faith. When the healing anointing is present, there is something imparted into your spirit man and there is a knowing inside you. When it is imparted, healing takes place instantly. Many of the healings of Jesus Christ are full-fledged, complete and instant healing and not partial healing. He could function that way because it was the gift of God freely given to people. In the same way when you are talking about faith you need to believe that you are healed by His stripes etc. and you need to believe that you have received. All these are important when talking about personal faith. But when the healing anointing comes, there is an impartation in your spirit man, and that you know that you know that something is done. It seems to contradict the word of faith message but if you believe for healing by faith you have to believe that it's already done and start giving thanks. But here we are taking about there is a knowing that comes saying that at the appointed time, the healing is going to manifest. This is what Jesus felt when the woman touched His garment -He knew something had happened. The woman too felt something happened when she touched Jesus. If you minister under the healing anointing, you need to know the anointing tangibly. If you receive healing under the healing anointing, you will feel something tangible. It is touchable -God comes down into the human realm to let us touch His power.

In Acts 4, I never understood why the apostles prayed like that because their prayer seemed to contradict the word of faith teaching. I want you to know that I am firmly grounded in the word of faith teaching. I believe and I confess all the promises of God. And under the faith teaching, I know that healing had already been done two thousand years ago. And I do know that in the New Testament, you don't ask God to heal under faith teaching because God has already done it by the stripes of Jesus. No point asking God what to do when He had already done so. But that faith teaching must be balanced, visa vis with the teaching on the healing anointing. In Acts 4, I want you to look at their prayer in verse 30 what they prayed there seemed to contradict the faith message at first. But if you understand the healing anointing, you know that their prayer doesn't contradict; it compliments. In other words, people need to understand faith all the time. They need to exercise faith all the time. But there is also a healing anointing which is a plus in what they can exercise. In verse 29 *Now, Lord, look on their threats, and grant to Your servants that with all boldness they may speak Your word.* They say, " God, give us boldness to speak Your word." How do you do that, in verse 30 it says by stretching Your hand to heal. How many of you know that God has a hand? When you minister by faith you don't pray, "*Jesus, heal*" but you say, "*Receive your healing.*" You don't ask Jesus to come and heal. But I want you to know that when Peter was in Lydia when he ministered there in Acts. 9:34 he used the present tense. Peter said to him "*Aeneas, Jesus the Christ heals*

113

you." He didn't say, *"Aeneas, by the stripes laid on Jesus you were healed."* But he is talking like Jesus has personally come. And I tell you He does when the healing anointing is released. I am not talking about exercising faith. Sometimes God wants you to receive by faith and not by the anointing. Now turn back to Acts 4 again to the same passage where we left off. Acts 4:30 by stretching out Your hand to heal. The healing anointing is when the hand of God comes and literally imparts faith.

49. THE APOSTOLIC ANOINTING

It worth exploring the divine truth that the distinguishing qualities of an apostle are evidenced by outstanding spiritual gifts, deep personal experience, power and ability to establish churches as well as the ability to provide adequate spiritual leadership. In order to have an in-depth understanding of the apostolic anointing, it is imperative that we first understand the apostolic office. The first distinguishing factor in apostleship is in *commission.* The most significant statement in the Bible regarding this office is that it was filled by Christ Himself. The Greek word *apostolos,* translated *"apostle,"* means "one sent forth, a sent one." Besides the first apostles to be commissioned on an apostolic mission, Jesus Christ is the greatest example of a sent one. In John 20:21, Jesus said to His disciples, *"Peace be unto you: as my father has sent me, even so I send you".* This tells me that a true apostle is always one with a commission—not one who merely goes, but one who is *sent.* A quintessential example is when Barnabas and Paul were sent forth to be apostles to the Gentiles (Acts 13:1). To cement this divine truth with ample scriptural evidence, in Acts 13:2, the Holy Spirit said, *"Separate me Saul* [Paul] *and Barnabas for the work to which I have called them."* It continues to say in verse 4, *"So they, being sent forth by the Holy Ghost, departed".* In other words, they were *"sent ones."* They left on their first missionary journey to the Gentiles.

The other distinguishing factor of apostleship is in *power or the ability to practically demonstrate signs and wonders.* Tapping on his own experience as an apostle, the apostle Paul himself speaks of the signs of an apostle, hence he writes: *Truly the signs of an* APOSTLE *were wrought among you in all patience, in signs, and wonders, and mighty deeds* (2 Corinthians 12:12). This tells me that in order to stand in this office, one must have a personal experience with the Lord—something very deep and real, something beyond the ordinary—not just something handed down by tradition but a direct personal encounter with God in the realm of the spirit. It comes out clear in the above-mentioned verse that the apostolic office is in *power* and not in the *name per se.* If the supernatural power is not there to back them up especially in establishing churches, then those involved are not real apostles. Don't get taken up with names and titles. If I didn't know what God called me to, I wouldn't fumble in the dark but if I sensed the call on the inside of me, I would preach and demonstate God's power and let God eventually set me in the office He has for me.

The other distinguishing mark of an apostle is in the depth of *revelation.* Paul said, in defending his apostleship, *"Am I not an apostle? Am I not free? Have I not seen Jesus Christ our Lord?"* (1 Corinthians 9:1). The phrase, *"Have I not seen Jesus Christ our Lord?"* connotes to his revelational encounter with the Lord Jesus in the realm of the spirit. In fact, Paul did not see Jesus in the flesh as the twelve did, but he saw Him through revelation (Acts 9:3-6). He had a deep spiritual experience with the Lord such that even his conversion was beyond the ordinary. In fact, Paul had such a deep spiritual experience with the Lord that he could say concerning what he knew about the Lord's Supper, *"For I have received of the Lord that which also I delivered unto you"* (1 Corinthians 11:23). The question is: How did he receive his teachings? Through revelation. Did you know that Paul didn't learn what he knew about this subject from the other apostles? Instead, he got it by revelation. Jesus directly gave it to him. Isn't it striking to note that Paul wasn't taught the Gospel he preached by man? The Spirit of God taught him. He wrote, *"But I certify you, brethren, that the gospel which was preached of me is not after man. For I neither received it of man, neither was I taught it, but by the revelation of Jesus Christ"* (Galatians 1:11, 12). It is therefore evident that the other way through which the apostolic anointing is unreservedly released from Heaven is through revelation. Revelation is the master key to unlocking the apostolic commission and an indispensable necessity for the one sent to demonstrate greater anointing.

In terms of function, the work of an apostle is that of a foundation layer: Paul testifies in 1 Corinthians 3:10 that *according to the grace of God which is given unto me, as a wise master builder, I have laid the foundation, and another buildeth thereon. But let every man take heed how he buildeth thereupon.*

In a related narrative, he contends in Ephesians 2:20 that *the Church is built upon the foundation of the apostles and prophets, Jesus Christ Himself being the chief corner stone.* It comes out clear in this respect that the first twelve apostles laid the foundation of the Church as the earliest pioneers and preachers of the Gospel. They also laid the foundation of the Church by receiving the Holy Spirit. The distinguishing result is *the ability to establish churches.* The apostle has the supernatural equipment called *"governments"* listed in 1 Corinthians 12:28. Weymouth translates it in modern language as *"powers of organization."* After churches are established, apostles can exercise authority over those churches they have established (1 Corinthians 9:1,2). Owing to lack of revelation, there are those who call themselves apostles because they want to dominate and rule people. They say, *"I'm an apostle. I have authority. You have to do what I say."* In New Testament days, the apostles could exercise authority only over the churches they had established themselves. Paul, for example, never exercised any authority over the church at Jerusalem or any of the churches other apostles had established. This tells me that you become an apostle over the churches that you yourself have established. A missionary who is really called of God and sent by the Holy Spirit is an apostle.

The other distinguishing quality of an apostle is that of being *a Jake of all trades* so to speak, as far as ministerial tasks are concerned. Notable is the realisation that an apostolic ministry seems to embrace all other ministry gifts. In other words, an apostle will have the ability of all the ministry gifts: He will do the work of the *evangelist*. He will get people saved. He will do the work of the *teacher*. He will teach and establish people. He will do the work of the *pastor*. He will pastor and shepherd people for a while. In studying closely the life of the Apostle Paul, we note that he said he never built on a foundation someone else had laid. He endeavoured to preach the Gospel where Christ was not named (Romans 15:20), and he always stayed in a place from six months to three years. His real calling was not to be a pastor, but he stayed long enough to get his converts established in the truth before moving on.

Owing to lack of revelation, some wonder if there are apostles today, citing tht the first apostles of Jesus Christ were the only apostles. This is gross ignorance of God's word because from these 12, came a breed of apostles sprouting right across generations. You see, initially, no one, not even Paul, could be an apostle in the sense the original twelve were. There are only *"twelve apostles of the Lamb"* (Revelation 21:14). Their qualifications were outlined in Acts 1, when the twelve selected an apostle to take Judas' place. We see from verses 21 and 22 that to be one of the twelve apostles of the Lamb, one had to have accompanied the apostles and Jesus during the entire time of His three and a half year ministry (Paul was not with them). Also, the original twelve were *"sent ones"* to be eyewitnesses of the ministry, works, life, death, burial, resurrection, and ascension of the Lord Jesus Christ. They stood in a place no other apostles or ministries can ever stand. There are, however, apostles today in the sense that Barnabas, Paul, and others were apostles. It says in Ephesians 4:11, *"And he gave some, apostles"* If God has taken this or any other ministry out of this list, then the Bible should have told us that He gave them for just a little while. All of the ministry gifts were given for the perfecting of the saints, the work of the ministry, and the edifying of the Body of Christ.

This includes apostles. Thank God, the office of the apostle exists today! For how long did God give the ministry gifts? According to verse 13, *all* of them were given,

"Till we all come in the unity of the faith, and of the knowledge of the Son of God unto a perfect man, unto the measure of the stature of the fullness of Christ."

If you think God called you to be an apostle, don't stress much about it. You won't start out there anyway. Paul didn't. Notice Barnabas and Paul were not set in the office of apostle to begin with, but God eventually did set them there. In Acts 13:1, it says, *"Now there were in the church that was at Antioch certain prophets and teachers; as Barnabas, Simeon, Lucius, Manaen and Saul."* Each of these men was either a prophet *or a* teacher, or a prophet and *a* teacher. Some may operate in more than one office—but a person doesn't operate in those offices as he wills. It is as God wills and as He anoints. Barnabas was a teacher. Saul (Paul) was a prophet and a teacher, for a prophet is one who has visions and revelations, and Paul received the entire Gospel that way. He would have been called a "seer" in the Old Testament, because he would see and know things supernaturally. As we have seen, in Acts 13:2 the Holy Spirit said, *"Separate me Barnabas and Saul for the work to which I have called them"* They had not yet gotten into the work that God called them to do. They fasted and prayed again, and the other ministers laid hands on them and sent them out, and they became apostles or missionaries to the Gentiles. Barnabas was considered an apostle as much as Paul was: *"Which when the apostles, Barnabas and Paul"* (Acts 14:14). In the city of Lystra, during this first missionary voyage, Paul ministered healing to a man who had been crippled from birth (Acts 14:8), and the people of the city wanted to worship Paul and Barnabas as gods, saying, *"The gods are come down to us in the likeness of men"* (verse 11). Paul and Barnabas had moved into another office that of apostle, and a stronger anointing had come, because it takes a stronger anointing to stand in that office. God rewards *faithfulness.* He doesn't reward *offices. A* prophet won't receive any more reward than a janitor who was faithful in his ministry of helps. Higher offices do not receive greater rewards; there is just a greater responsibility.

50. THE PASTORAL ANOINTING

In order for you to grasp a deeper revelation of the pastoral anointing, it is important that you first understand what the office of a pastor entails. It is striking to note that although it is the most overworked vocabulary in the Christian fratenity, the word *"pastor"* appears only once in The *King James*

Version. That's strikingly amazing, when it's the most popular and wide-spread office, more than any other office in the church today. The sole reference is in Ephesians 4:11 where it says, *"And He (God) gave some pastors."* However, we can find references to this office elsewhere in Scripture because the Greek word translated *"pastor"* also is translated *"shepherd."* Something else you need to understand to save you from confusion is the fact that the Greek word *episkopos* translated *"bishop"* is also translated *"overseer,"* for they are the same word. Both words also mean *"pastor."* In his farewell message to the elders, Paul said to the Church at Ephesus, *"Take heed therefore unto yourselves, and to all the flock, over the which the Holy Ghost hath made you overseers, to feed the church of God which he has purchased with his own blood"* (Acts 20:28). These elders were pastors. Great controversy has come concerning elders. Study Early Church history and you'll discover that the Greek word translated *"elder"* simply means "an older person." In the beginning days of the Church, they didn't have all of the ministries listed in the New Testament. The only ministries the Church had in the beginning were the apostles. Then came the great persecution in Jerusalem, and the early Christians were scattered abroad. They went everywhere preaching Jesus, and every one of them was a preacher. It is recorded in Acts 8:5 that *"Philip went down to Samaria and preached Christ unto them."* But Philip was not an evangelist then. The apostles had laid hands on him and he was set into the office of deacon first.

It comes out clear that later, in the 21st chapter of Acts, that Luke and Paul and their company went down to Caesarea and were in the house of *"Philip the evangelist."* When God began to raise up ministries, He made an evangelist out of Philip. It takes time to develop ministries. You may get saved—and even baptized in the Holy Spirit—today, and the call of God may be on you to be a pastor, but you'll have to be prepared for it. So, start out to obey God, whether you're in the ministry or not, and God will promote you and use you in a greater way. If you, like Philip, learn to be faithful wherever you are, God may see fit to move you on. If He does, fine. If He doesn't, just stay faithful where you are. He'll not be able to use you fully if you're not faithful. In the Early Church, because there was a lack of ministries, they would appoint an elder ("an older person") over a particular flock. Out of these elders God developed pastors or overseers. It is certainly unscriptural to take a layman who has no anointing upon him and put him in the office of an elder or make him overseer of a congregation because he doesn't have the anointing to do it. He only has an anointing like any other believer. So, we see that the *bishop, overseer,* or *elder* is the same office: the *pastoral* office. Who has the oversight of the flock? The shepherd does. What does *"shepherd"* mean? The Greek word translated *"shepherd"* is translated *"pastor."* Who, then, would oversee the flock? The shepherd

118

would. Jesus is called by Peter *"the Shepherd and Bishop of your souls"* (1 Peter 2:25). And in First Peter 5:4 we read, *"And when the chief shepherd shall appear, ye shall receive a crown of glory that fadeth not away."* Jesus is the Great Shepherd, the Chief Shepherd, of all God's sheep, Jesus, has under shepherds. A pastor is an under shepherd of God's sheep. God calls and equips men to shepherd, or pastor, a flock.

51. THE EVANGELICAL ANOINTING

An evangelical anointing is one of the most powerful anointings which God has bequeathed upon believers in the Body of Christ since the main business of the church is winning souls. In order for us to understand how to operate and flow in the anointing for Evangelism, we must first understand what Evangelism is as one of the five-fold ministry offices. The Webster's Seventh New Collegiate Dictionary defines Evangelism as *the act of winning or revival of personal commitments to Christ.* In laymen's terms, it is the winning of people to Jesus Christ for salvation. An Evangelist is a person who goes from place preaching the Gospel of Jesus Christ for the conversion of souls. The Greek word for Evangelist is *euaggelistes* pronounced *yoo-ang-ghel-is-tace* which means a preacher of the Gospel. The Evangelism Anointing is a supernatural ability to preach the Gospel of Jesus Christ with signs following, including healing, and deliverance, which results in the salvation of souls.

The Word of God also talks about the office of the exhorter (Romans 12:8). We usually think of exhortation as being part of all these other offices, but there is a specific office of exhorter. Those whom we call *"evangelists"* often are exhorters. The word *"evangelist,"* however, is used only three times in the New Testament: Firstly, *"Philip the evangelist"* is spoken of in Acts 21:8. Secondly, the gift *"evangelist"* is listed in Ephesians 4:11 and lastly, Paul told Timothy to do *"the work of an evangelist"* In 2 Timothy 4:5, Philip, then, is the only model other than Jesus that we have for an evangelist. In the early days of the Church, we see that Philip went down to Samaria and preached with great miracles resulting. At that time, however, as we will study in Chapter 8, Philip was still a deacon. In Acts 8:5-7 5 it says,

"Philip went down to the city of Samaria, and preached Christ unto them.

And the people with one accord gave heed unto those things which Philip spoke, hearing and seeing the miracles which he did. For unclean spirits, crying with loud voice, came out of many that were possessed with them: and many taken with palsies, and that were lame, were healed".

Practical Denmonstrations Of The Anointing

There's no doubt Philip was anointed by the Holy Spirit. Many who were lame were healed. It doesn't mention anything about anybody else being healed, but those healings were enough to attract attention to Jesus. People got saved, *"and there was great joy in that city"* (verse 8). Luke 10:1 and chapter 10 verses 17-19 also gives us this example that we should follow. It is recorded that Jesus called His twelve disciples together, and gave them power and authority over all devils, and to cure diseases. And he sent them to preach the Kingdom of God, and to heal the sick. And he said unto them,

"Take nothing for your journey, neither staves, nor scrip, neither bread, neither money; neither have two coats apiece. And whatsoever house ye enter into, there abide, and thence depart. And whosoever will not receive you, when ye go out of that city, shake off the very dust from your feet for a testimony against them."

And they departed, and went through the towns, preaching the gospel, and healing everywhere. It is evident that many people will not believe the Word because signs are not following our preaching, as an evidence and proof of the authenticity of the Word of God that we are presenting. But when those with the Evangelism Anointing preach to Muslims, Hindus, atheist, and other non-believers, with supernatural evidence of signs following, multitudes of them will turn to Jesus Christ for salvation. The greater truth is that we can't try to reason them to Christ, for they consider our reasoning as just another opinion. We must have signs as a proof of the Word of God that we are presenting to them. Paul testifies in Corinthians 2:4-5 saying;

And my speech and my preaching was not with enticing words of man's wisdom, but in demonstration of the Spirit and power: That your faith should not stand in the wisdom of men, but in the power of God.

Notable is the realisation that most of God's anointings comes by first qualifying, through ministering faithfully in an area of ministry. This was the case with Philip the Deacon turned Evangelist. Acts 6:1-7 gives what most believe is his charge to become a Deacon, in which he helped in the natural by ministering to the physical needs of widows. In Acts 21:8, we see the first mention of Evangelist, and it is referring to this same Philip. It is evident that an evangelist tells the Good News (the Gospel) to unbelievers. This is what defines the distinction between *teaching* and *preaching* (Acts 28:31). The clear-cut difference is in both the message and its constituency. True preaching contains in it, the message of salvation, and speaks to the unbeliever, while teaching is mostly directed to the believer, to deepen his understanding of the Bible. When we read Mark 16:15-18, we see that verse 15 sets the tone of this scripture as evangelistic. The signs that follow are the evidence or proof of the preaching of the Gospel of Jesus Christ. Mark

16:15 says; *And he said unto them, Go ye into all the world, and preach the gospel to every creature.* Verses 17-18 are the evidences or results of the preaching of the Gospel, it reads:

"And these signs shall follow them that believe; In my name shall they cast out devils; they shall speak with new tongues; They shall take up serpents; and if they drink any deadly thing, it shall not hurt them; they shall lay hands on the sick, and they shall recover."

This scripture gives us the evidence that should be manifested as we preach the Gospel of Jesus Christ to every creature. Philip believed in Jesus name, and these proofs were evident when he preached the Gospel of Jesus Christ. You too, should expect these same results. Again, in Mark 16:20 it shows us that when we preach the Word, God confirms the Word preached with signs following, it reads; *And they went forth, and preached every where, the Lord working with them, and confirming the word with signs following. Amen.* The key to the Evangelistic anointing is the preaching of the Word of God, expecting and believing that God will confirm the Word with signs. Signs are the results of Evangelistic preaching. Signs were the results that Philip the Evangelist saw manifested after his preaching, The Evangelism anointing can enable you to preach publicly aloud, amongst many people, or privately, to one person or just a few. It is not just the volume of the person speaking that makes it preaching, rather the content of the message, which is salvation through Jesus Christ and repentance. The Evangelism anointing is not meant to sit amongst the Saints, rather to go out to the world with demonstration and power. This anointing is not a passive anointing, rather an active one, not an anointing of words alone, but the demonstration of God's power.

52. THE ADMINISTRATIVE ANOINTING

The Bible speaks of the gifts of administration, hence there is an anointing that comes as a package with this grace. In a modern day Church context, administration has more to do with the efficient organisation, coordination and facilitation of church activities in order to expedite God's plans and purpose with Heavenly efficiency. It also entails administering the business affairs of the church in order to spearhead and propagate the gospel of the Lord Jesus Christ to the extreme ends of the world. The administrative anointing, or the lack thereof, can either make or break any church or ministry. The truth is that if you can preach to fifty, then you can preach to five thousand. What makes the difference is how many can you administer! In business, it is said that secretaries run the company and so it is with spiritual organisations; administrators run the show, although behind the scenes. The anointing to effectively administer people, resources and money is the crucial factor in the success of any organized endeavour in the Kingdom. The administrative anointing is unveiled in the scripture below:

*And God hath set some in the church, first apostles, secondarily prophets, thirdly teachers, after that miracles, then gifts of healings, helps, **governments**, diversities of tongues* (1 Corinthians 12:28).

In the context of the above-mentioned scripture, the term, *"governments"*, connotes to the administrative anointing. Philosophically speaking, apostles and prophets plough the ground, teachers and evangelists seed the ground, but helps and governments pick, process and protect the fruit. Helps and governments are anointings to be honoured for the vital role they play. Testimonies are the dessert in the meal of spiritual leaders everybody loves to be vindicated, but the administrators and the intercessors who work behind the scenes share in the fruit. In fact, they are the key to the spiritual leader's success. The spiritual leader must seek to promote joy and blessing among those who administrate the success of their ministry. Cohesion comes out of communication and clarity of vision, with love and joy being the fuel of unity. Someone once said that people don't care about how much you know, until they know how much you care. The spiritual leader must fully care for those who are his helps and governments. It is therefore imperative that administrators execute divine tasks with Heavenly efficiency. Consider the following scripture:

And whatsoever you do, do it heartily, as to the Lord, and not unto men (Colossians 3:23).

This infers that when you learn to perceive or feel God's heart in everything you do in ministry, you are beginning to flow in the administrative anointing. The administrative anointing must be honoured, and set to the highest standards, for the glory of God and the advancement of His Kingdom. The gifts of the Spirit flow in those who are filled with great grace and love. God can, and does, give revelation about correct email addresses, ledger statements, and all of the myriad details of life and ministry, because they are all important, vital details in His Kingdom.

53.THE KINGLY ANOINTING

The Kingly anointing is the grace or supernaturally ability imparted upon a man to lead, govern and control others in the Kingdom. This anointing comes with greater responsibility in the Kingdom. In a modern day context, men of God who have a responsibility over geographical territories around the world have a Kingly anointing to govern those territories on behalf of the Kingdom. Saul and David had a Kingly anointing although Saul later on lost that anointing. The Kingly anointing comes after one has occupied the office of as King because it is a governmental anointing. Let's make reference to how Kings were ordained into the Kingly office in the olden days:

> *Then Samuel took the vial of oil and poured it on Saul's head and kissed him and said, has not the Lord anointed you to be prince over His heritage Israel?* (1 Samuel 10:1).

It is evident that the Kingly Anointing is what ushered people into the office of a king. It is the Anointing that turned an ordinary person into the King of Israel. The two greatest examples of the Kingly Anointing are seen in the lives of David and Saul. You will notice how King Saul rose to a place of authority through the Anointing. The Lord sent Samuel to Anoint Saul, an ordinary person. You will see how Saul was completely transformed into a different person and was exalted because of the Anointing.

However, the Kingly anointing did not end in the Old Testament. While in the Old Testament it was only restricted to few individuals, following the resurrection of the Lord Jesus Christ from the dead, now every believer is called to be a King and a Priest in the Kingdom. Consider what Paul had to say concerning this spiritual reality:

> *God has called us to be Kings and Priests unto Him. And from Jesus Christ the faithful and trustworthy Witness, the Firstborn of the dead [first to be brought back to life] and the Prince (Ruler) of the kings of the earth. To Him Who ever loves us and has once [for all] loosed and freed us from our sins by His own blood, 6And formed us into a kingdom (a royal race), priests to His God and Father--to Him be the glory and the power and the majesty and the dominion throughout the ages and forever and ever. Amen (so be it)* (Revelation 1:5-6).

It is only by the Anointing that you will fulfil this calling to authority and true Kingship.

> *For if because of one man's trespass (lapse, offense) death reigned through that one, much more surely will those who receive [Gods] overflowing grace (unmerited favour) and the free gift of righteousness [putting them into right standing with Himself] REIGN AS KINGS in life through the one man Jesus Christ (the Messiah, the Anointed One)* (Romans 5:17).

Nothing can compare with the Kingly Anointing. This powerful anointing lifts a person to place of high authority in God. Basing his experience on the Kindly anointing, David once testified saying,

What is man, that you are mindful of him? or the son of man, that you visit him? You have made him a little lower than the angels; You have crowned him with glory and honour, and set him over the works of Your hands

(Hebrews 2:7)

It is every born-again man and women who has the potential to walk in Kingdom dominion that the writer of Hebrews is speaking of. In the natural realm, there are Kings who govern nations. Many prime ministers and presidents in the nations of the world are actually standing in the office of a King. These political Kings hold the positions and power to lead, influence and shape the economy, development, and course of entire nations. In a broader sense Kings are usually the people at the top--the best the champions, the leaders in their respective fields. However, while natural Kings govern the natural realm, we as Kings and Priest in the Kingdom, govern the spiritual realm which directly influence the natural realm. So, in the order of God, we are above Kings of the natural realm, for we are seated with Christ in the Heavenly places, which speaks of an elevated position of authority and power in the whole Universe.

"And He has on His robe and on His thigh a name written: king of kings and lord of lords." (Revelation 19:16).

The Kingly anointing is an anointing for ruling and reigning. It is an anointing for dominion and government. It is also an anointing for prevailing. It has strength and might to push back the forces of darkness and take new ground. This mighty anointing enables one to break through. This record-breaking anointing will enable them to break certain records within their own locality, city, country, or sphere of influence. However, not many can handle such an anointing or hold on securely to the Kingly office. King Saul couldn't. He attained, but could not maintain the position because he did not have the character to contain it. Sadly, many in ministry fall not long after receiving this powerful and authoritative anointing. Therefore, God in His wisdom and love will not bestow this Kingly anointing on just anyone, nor will He simply bequeath it to the unprepared. The preparations for the ministry of Kings are usually extensive and intensive. And it usually involves seasons of breaking and times of brokenness. That's the main reason why God allowed David to dwell in the caves and wilderness for a rather lengthy season before He elevated David to the palace.

124

> *"Now when the Philistines heard that they had anointed David king over Israel, all the Philistines went up to search for David. And David heard of it and went down to the stronghold"* (1 Samuel 5:17).

It is easier to enter such an office than to hold it in an enduring manner. It takes special grace, wisdom, authority, strength, and the blessing and mercy of God to hold such an office---especially the office of a King! The Kingly anointing is one of the most powerful anointings that an individual can possibly carry. There is perhaps only one other mightier anointing which a mortal can carry - *the weighty Glory anointing.* The anointing emanates from one's whole being when he or she is clothed in the weighty glory! There are those in the Kingdom who are carrying a measure of this weight, and are being prepared in the crucible of pressure. Those who consistently develop and carry this strong anointing will become high achievers, accomplish mighty deeds, slay giants and rise up to become spiritual champions.

The Kingdom anointing is very powerful and poses a great threat to the realm of darkness. The enemy will go all out to prevent one from breaking into and getting established in this higher level of anointing. The enemy will mount the fiercest spiritual attacks and put up the most stubborn obstruction in the lives of those who have just received this anointing. The early and pre-emptive attacks, obstructions, and distractions are intended to prevent one from fully transitioning into the new anointing and from being established as king. Once a person is established, set and firmly planted in this anointing, there will be a stability and strength that the enemy finds more difficult to come against.

> *"So David knew that the Lord had established him as king over Israel, and that He had exalted His kingdom for the sake of His people Israel."* (2 Samuel 5:12).

When Paul spoke of being seated with Christ in the Heavenly places, he alluded to a Kingly position of authority and power. Every believer is called, chosen and ordained to be Kings. Between the calling and the ordaining is the proving ground that will determine whether one wears the royal crown. Just because one is ordained into a specific calling does not mean they are automatically chosen to operate in the Kingly anointing. Although many have received the kingly calling and are destined for the throne, they may not actually succeed in being confirmed and crowned as kings. They will not be crowned unless they allow the potential, anointing, and call in their lives to develop and they have proven themselves worthy. Many potential Kings have not pursued their call and failed to fulfil their full destiny. These may not fully realize that their failure to pursue and enter into their full destiny will not only deprive themselves of priceless blessings and glory, but many others would also be deprived of the blessings that could have flowed through their kingly ministry.

Joseph is another quintessential example of one who functioned under the Kingly anointing. When Joseph fulfilled his destiny, he saved many lives, including his own family, during a very severe famine which lasted seven long years (Genesis 41-47). People from the surrounding nations came to Egypt to seek his assistance. When Esther fulfilled her destiny, she was instrumental in saving her people from mass genocide. When Jesus Christ fulfilled His destiny by sacrificing Himself on the cross, He made it possible for all men that believed in Him to receive forgiveness and salvation. Do not underestimate what can result from a single person's obedience to the call of God and fulfilment of his destiny. God will entrust this high office only to those who have proven their faithfulness in the things of God. Faithfulness is the quality that God is looking for in those who will be entrusted with the Kingship and ruler-ship. We receive greater authority only when we submit to the ultimate authority, the King of Kings.

"Behold, I am coming quickly! Hold fast what you have, that no one may take your crown." (Revelation 3:11).

In the book of Revelation, the 24 Elders cast down their crowns (a symbol of Kingship) before the King of Kings. To the King of Kings, all the other Kings must prostrate fall!

"Now why do you cry aloud? Is there no King in your midst?" (Micah 4:9).
"Where the word of a King is, there is power?"" (Ecclesiastic 8:4).

It is scripturally evident that where there is a scarcity of Kings, the church will experience logistic problems and the opposite is true. When some abdicated Kings refuse their calling, or if an evil King is ruling, a vital supply to the Body of Christ is cut off. One cannot function adequately in the Kingly office without first receiving the Kingly anointing. Kings have the anointing, authority and power to declare and decree in the spirit. Things happen when they exercise this authority under the anointing. The spirit and angelic realm recognizes and responds to true spiritual authority and anointing. Demons and angels will not respond to those who are grandstanding on their Kingly authority to make decrees over the nations. It is for this reason that the Bible concurs in Job 22:28 that:

126

"You will also declare (decree) a thing, and it will be established for you; so light will shine on your ways."

God made David a commander over His people. Kings are commanders-in-chief. In some measure, they have the power and authority to command and order things to be done. There will be times, provided the judgment is right and needed urgently, when Kings will need to command and decree instead of wasting hours, days, weeks, and even months trying to debate and seek consensus on every insignificant policy. The person who is obligated to explain everything to everyone every time is not a king. There are times when hesitation, indecisiveness, and failure to exert one's authority will result in major losses and defeat. Therefore, there will be times when a King has to act decisively and swiftly.

"Behold many Kings shall be raised up from the ends of the earth." (Jeremiah 50:41).

The gospel of John portrays Jesus as the Son of God and is symbolized by the eagle. In this Third Day, we shall have more revelation concerning Christ the King as revealed in the gospel of Matthew and symbolized by the face of a lion. The ministry and manner of Kings shall be manifested more and more in this dispensation than in the ages past. For in this Third Millennium, many Kings of the Lord shall be raised up from the ends of the earth. When these Kings begin to stand in their office, and when they begin to fulfil their function faithfully, we shall see more rapid and forceful advancements in the Kingdom of God on earth. The powerful, influential, and strategic Kingly ministry is most needed for such a time as this, a time when so many things in this world move at an accelerated pace, a time of great uncertainty which calls for sharp discernment and bold leadership.

54. THE PRIESTLY ANOINTING OR INTERCESSORY ANOINTING

In the Old Testament, God would call a King and a Priest into an office and then impart an anointing associated with these offices. It is worth mentioning that every believer is called to a priestly ministry of prayer. It's not for the so called prayer warriors but an irrevocable inheritance bequeathed upon every believer in Christ. There are few things that need to be given divine correction pertaining to the ministry of intercession. Intercessory prayer is not a laundry list of requests. Intercession is not about making faithless, beggarly prayers as Heaven does not understand that kind of language. Intercession is not about pleading a cause and getting answers. We don't just get answers to our prayers - we become the answers because the world requires Heavens' solutions and not google answers. In other words, we gain knowledge and insight into solutions, hence we become a solution to the cries of millions across the globe.

The priestly anointing is the ability to stand on the gap on behalf of others. In the Old Testament, priests used to stand on behalf of people and make sacrifices one every year in the Holy of Holies. However, since the old covenant has been done away with, the priestly anointing is now an intercessory anointing that comes upon those who would go an extra mile to stand in the gap in prayer. While dozens of believers are inclined towards prayers of supplication in which they beg and petition God to respond to their cries, the most effective intercessory prayer in the realm of the spirit is prophetic declaration. It involves stepping up to your level of sonship in Christ to decree what you want to see happen in your world. It involves changing the situations and circumstances of your life by the words you speak. However, between prophetic *declaration* and *manifestation*, you need to put yourself into a *"prophetic process"* called *intercession*, which is a birthing position in which you align your spirit to give birth to the prophetic word in the realm of the spirit. Intercession aligns our spirit and causes us to be rightly positioned in the spirit dimension so as to swiftly move, function and operate in the realm of the spirit.

It's important that after declaring the word, we must enter into prayer or intercession so as to birth forth a manifestation in the physical realm.

This was exemplified by Elijah who got down and put himself into a birthing position and prayed until a cloud as small as a man's hand appeared over the horizon and suddenly abundant rain started precipitating heavily after a long period of drought (1 Kings 18:42). The prophecy is what gave life to it but the intercession is what caused it to grow until it was birthed forth. I'm reminded of what John Wesley, the great man of God once said, *"I pray for two hours every morning, that is if I don't have a lot to do. If I have a lot to do that day, I pray for three hours"*.

55. THE TEACHING ANOINTING

This is the grace and ability to teach the word, unpack and unveil the deep mysteries of God encapsulated in the word. Kenneth Hagin says even though he wasn't a teacher to begin with, he always had the greatest respect for the Word of God, and always was very studious. This is what he had to say:

> *"I spent hours studying and reading, digging things out for myself in my early years as a pastor, but I didn't teach those things. I had no unction or leading to teach. I did teach a Bible class in the church, however. Kenneth Hagin says just standing there with a handful, teaching them the Word, the anointing would come on me so strongly I couldn't stand it. I'd have to say, "Lord, turn it off—I can't stand it anymore!" It was like getting hold of electric current. That anointing and the Word flowed out to the people.*

It is important to understand that for you to flow in the teaching anointing, you must have the ingredient of revelation. Revelation is the mind of God revealed to humanity which enables him to see beyond the confines of the dimensions of space, distance, time and matter. It is knowledge beyond mere memorisation of scriptures but spiritual perception of nuggets of spiritual truths and divine insights emanating straight from the throne room of heaven. It is the knowledge of God revealed to our spirits and is received by spiritually seeing, hearing and perceiving in the realm of the spirit. When God speaks directly to a man's spirit and that man understands what was said, that activity is what the Bible calls *"revelation"* knowledge. It is the mind of God revealed so that mankind could exercise dominion over time, space and matter. God can only be known by revelation hence in the context of the scripture above, to **know God** therefore means to have a revelation of who God says He is, what He says He has, what He says He has done and what He says He can do. . This is what culminates in unprecedented torrents of explosive power. It is worth unveiling the divine truth that knowledge that is received or transmitted through reason brings one under a curse, while knowledge that is received or transmitted through revelation brings one under a blessing. God's Original Design for Man to Live out of Revelation Knowledge. In the spirit realm things are not taught but they are revelaed. God never meant men to study hard but just to be catapulted into a realm where things are supernaturally revelaed to them.

Paul is one of the greatest teachers who ever lived in this world. What makes him great is the fact that his teachings were loaded with revelation from the Throne Room of Heaven. Unlike Jesus' twelve disciples, the apostle Paul did not have a personal relationship with Christ before His resurrection. The message he preached was totally based upon the "revelation" knowledge that Paul received directly from the Holy Spirit. Paul wrote in Galatians 1:11-12,

Practical Demonstrations Of The Anointing

"But I certify you, brethren, that the gospel which was preached of me is not after man. For I neither received it of man, neither was I taught it, but by <u>revelation</u> ("apokalupsis") of Jesus Christ."

For this reason, the epistles Paul wrote are teeming with "revelation" knowledge about spiritual truth that is unsurpassed by the other New Testament authors in both depth and insight. Paul possessed a comprehension of spiritual wisdom that was far ahead of his contemporaries. Trench's Lexicon says that revelation (*"apokalupsis"*) means an uncovering, a laying bare, a disclosure of truth, instruction, concerning Divine things before unknown. It includes not merely the thing shown and seen, but the interpretation or unveiling of the same, given by God Himself through the operation of the Holy Spirit. These "spiritual" truths were available to each of the Lord's disciples; but Paul was the one who paid the price to receive them. The book of Galatians tells us that Paul separated himself from people for several years (Galatians 1:16-24), and sought the Lord through prayer and through intense study of God's Word. Because Paul had not personally witnessed the crucifixion and resurrection of Christ, he was not encumbered with sense knowledge reasoning and mental logic when he interpreted their meaning. The *"revelation"* knowledge that He received directly from the Lord was, therefore, pure and not restricted by mental prejudice. He wrote what the Lord revealed to him. He believed what God told him..

The Apostle Peter said that some of the things Paul wrote were hard to understand by the carnal and religious mind; but, nevertheless, they were reliable and just as trustworthy as the rest of scripture. II Peter 3:15-16,

"...our beloved brother Paul also according to the wisdom given unto him hath written unto you. As also in all his epistles, speaking in them of these things; in which are some things hard to be understood, which they that are unlearned and unstable wrest, as they do also the other scriptures, unto their own destruction."

Paul also believed that every believer, irrespective of his previous education or past life, has the same potential that he had to receive "revelation" knowledge directly from the mouth of God. Paul wrote in I Timothy 2:4 that fully describes God's intent for all mankind, *"Who will have all men to be saved, and to come unto the <u>knowledge</u> ("epignosis") of the truth."* The Amplified Bible says that *"God wishes all men to be saved and [increasingly] to perceive and recognize and discern and know precisely and correctly the [Divine] Truth."* It is God's will for every man and every woman of faith to receive and to comprehend "*revelation*" knowledge. It is therefore evident that God designed man to be a daily recipient of revelation knowledge. In the Garden of Eden, man walked and talked with God. Adam and Eve were receiving revelation knowledge daily from Almighty God. Jesus also demonstrated this lifestyle of doing nothing out of His own initiative, but only what He heard and saw the Father doing (John 5:19,20,30).

56. THE DELIVERANCE ANOINTING

It is important to highlight from the onset the fact that although casting of devils is a central theme in the deliverance ministry, this ministry isn't about demons! It's about guiding and helping the masses come into the victory that Christ died to give them! The purpose of ministering deliverance is to set free those who are in bondage. As Jesus was sent forth to preach deliverance to the captives (Luke 4:18), decaring that "*The Spirit of the Lord is upon me, because he has anointed me to preach deliverance to the captives...*"), so we are also sent out (John 20:21). Then said Jesus to them, "*as my Father has sent me, even so send I you.*" to do the works He did (John 14:12), "*He that believes in me, the works that I do shall he do also...*"), and this includes casting out of devils (Matthew 10:8). The ministry of deliverance is about bringing spiritual victory and freedom to those who are in bondage. It doesn't matter what you call it (demonized, possessed, oppressed, etc.), if they are in demonic bondage, whether they need to tear down a stronghold, break up a legal ground, cast a demon out, or all three, it's still deliverance, because it's setting the captives free. Casting out demons, is just part of the overall ministry of deliverance.

This is the grace or ability to cast out demons, dismantle satanic strongholds and liberate the masses. However, this does not mean that there is a special breed of people who should cast out demons because casting out devils is a grace given to everybody. However, what I am talking about here is a dimension or level of operation. There are those who seem to be excelling in this ministry because they have received a greater measure of grace to undertake it. This is where I see some deliverance ministries miss the mark. They think it's as simple as commanding the demon to come out, and there's nothing more they can do. This is a grave mistake that causes a lot of people to walk away from a deliverance still in bondage. There is more to it than simply casting out demons. In Luke 9:42, we are told a story of how Jesus not only rebuked demons in a boy who was mentally affected by evil spirits, but also is said to have healed the boy. There is no mention of the boy needing physical healing, but if you look up the word healed in this passage, one of the meanings is, *"to free from errors and sins"*, which is likely what Jesus did with the boy, Jesus removed the boy's legal grounds (sins) and freed him from errors (strongholds). This case of deliverance required more then just rebuking demons!

There have been times when I have successfully helped people out of their demonic bondages, without even having to cast out demons! Sometimes all that is needed is the pulling down of a stronghold, or a breaking up of a legal right. Other times, all three areas need to be addressed to bring the person into complete freedom. Every deliverance minister should be knowledgeable with all three of these very important elements, and be prepared to address them without hesitation:

Tearing down strongholds: Strongholds are incorrect thinking patterns that people develop over time, and are often set up and nurtured by demons through lies and deception. Demons thrive on strongholds, and use them to hang around a person and torment them. You need to have a clear insight into exactly what a stronghold is, and how to go about tearing them down. Failing to tear down strongholds can hold up a deliverance and prevent us from walking in complete spiritual freedom.

- **Removing legal rights:** Legal rights are things that give demons permission to enter and remain in our lives. Before demons can often be cast out, it is important to address and remove these legal rights. Failing to remove legal rights can hold up a deliverance very easily.

- **Inner healing:** Many times when a person has been abused, rejected, wounded, or hurt in some way, there is an emotional wound that needs to be healed. Demons will use these wounds and weaknesses against the person, as leverage to hold them in bondage and get them to re-open doors so that they can re-enter. Inner healing is a vital step in the overall restoration process that needs to take place in the lives of many who are seeking deliverance.

- **Casting out the demons:** This requires two basic elements: knowledge of your authority in Christ Jesus over the powers of the enemy, and faith in that authority. Demons are cast out with a simple spoken command, such as, *"I command the spirit of fear to come out in the name of Jesus!"* and instantly, they vacate the body into perpetuity.

57. THE WORSHIP OR MUSICAL ANOINTING

This is the ability to worship God deeeply, accurately, truthfully and spiritu-ally. While God has created everybody to worship him, there are those who God impart a grace to lead others into the greater depths of His presence. The musical anointing is the ability to compose worship songs that extol the father. It is the ability to usher the presence of God in a scene through wor-ship. It is of paramount significance that we define worship and see what the essence of worship fully entails. This is because so many believers are involved in worship activities but somehow lack a revelation of what wor-ship really is. Worship is all that we are responding to all that He is. Webster dictionary defines worship as *an act of paying homage to a dignitary or somebody higher than you.* In a spiritual sense, it is a divine act of adoration, honour and reverence directed to God, the bases of which is His Word, which is a vehi-cle by which a man pours out all his heart to Him. In a deeper sense, it is a direct contact between the human spirit and the Holy Spirit in the realm of the spirit, the result of which the *lesser spirit* is yielded, mingled and infused into the *Greater one*, culminating in what we call the *drinking together of spirits.* In other words, your spirit is flowing into the Holy Spirit in the same way the waters of a river are ushered into the sea. From a scientific point of view, unless and if the terminals (positive and negative) contact each other, there is no flow of current. By the same token, unless your spirit has con-tacted the Holy Spirit during worship, you have not worshipped at all. To understand the true essence of worship, let's look closely at the revelation that is gleaned in the narrative in John 4, when Jesus spoke to the Samaritan woman at the well.

It is worth exploring the truth that presenting yourself as a vessel of wor-ship is the key to accessing the higher realms of God's glory. In worship, we experience the original atmosphere of the glory God intended us to be in with Him. Worship is an atmosphere or realm in which we were given birth to by God before His throne in Heaven. Therefore, when we worship God, we are home seek as we long to be in this very original atmosphere of glory He created us in. In worship, you are not concerned with the elements of matter because God becomes the matter you worship for *without Him was not anything made that was made* (John 1:3). He is everything that is and is to be, all the while waiting for us to simply worship who He is. Oxygen is to a natural man what worship correspondingly is to a spiritual man. During worship, God inhales our worship and He exhales His glory. Hence, worship is a *di-vine transaction,* so to speak. That is why there is such a thing as the *transaction of the glory,* meaning the pouring out of our very being in exchange with the breath of life from God's presence. In the very breath of God is where you will find the atmosphere ripe for the miraculous. That's where you find the supernatural mass that provokes a torrent of miracles, signs and wonders to break out, culminating in a perennial stream flow of praise and worship to the Father.

However, it is disheartening to note that most believers have not fully comprehended the difference between *praise* and *worship*. The difference between praise and worship is that praise is an affirmation of God's works while worship is an affirmation of God's presence. Prophetically speaking, God said, "*Worship is an affirmation of My presence, that is why when I am affirmed, I have to manifests Myself*". We praise God for what He has done but we worship Him for who He is. The Praiser says to God,

"Lord I thank you for my lucrative job, amazing family, blooming business and all that you have blessed me with" but the Worshiper says, *"Lord, I worship you for who you are, even if I don't have anything, you are God, you mean so much to me, You are the King of Kings and Lords of Lords"*.

Therefore, praise is the proclamation of the great and powerful works of God expressed by singing, playing musical instruments and giving shouts of joy as well as by different postures of the body such as clapping, dancing and raising hands. Notable is the realisation that praise is not about singing the fast–tempo songs that makes you dance, jump and shout. Neither does worship imply the slow paced songs that people sing emotionally and present as a prelude to the preaching of the word. Instead, praise is an exuberant, clamorous and enthusiastic expression that often includes many words and a physical display. Worship on the other hand involves fewer words, at times no words are needed at all as there is total silence because it has more to do with inwardly pouring out our hearts before God. I'm reminded of how Hannah poured out her spirit in worship before God such that words could not come out although her silence spoke louder than her weeping. This is the essence of true worship. She worshiped God so deeply to the extent that her worship was mistaken by the Priest as drunkenness. You see, there are times when you are so absorbed, mingled and infused in an atmosphere of worship such that even those around you will think you are out of your mind. It is worth exploring the divine truth that the greatest depths of worship are reached without uttering any meaningful words to the mind. Did you know that every element of nature or creation emits deep sounds of worship to God, even without uttering a single word? That is why the Bible says *Heavens declare the glory of God and the stars and the moon proclaim the work of His hands.* This is to tell you that there is silent communication taking place between God and His creation during worship, even without any sounds, voices or words emitted. David, a man who understood the depths of worship more than any other person in the past generations concur in Psalms 148 that *God commands the moon, sun and stars to praise Him.* But in essence, how can the moon, sun and stars praise God? This is because all creation has the ability to hear, listen, obey and respond and worship the Creator. Even inanimate objects respond in worship to Him. Often, we listen to music and worship tapes to help us get into the presence of God because music is the international sound of the earth but when you are outdoors, in touch with creation, you sense God's presence without man-made music because there is a natural on-going orchestra of worship via the creation. Did you know that rock samples from distant planets emit sounds of worship that we can hear when put under special machines that track sound waves and energy? The truth is that creation emits sound waves of worship that are invisible to your ear but your spirit receives them.

It is an incontestable reality that worship is the highest form of intimacy with God. This is because worship brings us into the third Heaven, right before the Throne Room of God. That is why in worship, we experience the atmosphere of Heaven on earth. Worship is the catalyst that brings about the substance of Glory from God's Throne down to the earth. Therefore, true worship opens the new Heavenly sound in the earth, a sweet melody resonating from your innermost being and not just the mimic of worship from your flesh. The greater truth is that as we worship corporately, we build a supernatural mass such that as our worship intensifies, along with the sound of all those around us worshiping, the sound gains mass. As that mass of worship takes on more energy, it begins to lift the entire group of worshipers into another realm, the glory realm. That is why the greatest miracles are expected to happen during worship. It's because miracles are within the mass of His presence which is known as the *glory.* During ministration, we therefore speak into that mass and then the mass takes on the word we speak and miracles happen. The reason why we don't see miracles as we ought to in the church today is because there is not enough mass in the service to manifest miracles. The truth is that the realm of worship is the realm of the miraculous. In other words, miracles and worship goes hand in glove just like praise and worship. If you can praise, it's easy to enter the realm of worship. By the same token, if you worship long and deep enough, it's easy to enter the realm of the miraculous. The truth is that when we worship God, the eternal become our reality and the impossible becomes our possibility. Can you imagine the day when we would worship and every wheelchair is emptied, every blind eye is opened, every deaf ear is opened, every cancer-ridden body is healed and every death victim is raised from the dead? This is the true essence of worship which shall become a common occurrence in the Body of Christ in these end times.

CHAPTER SEVEN

A SEVEN-FOLD PROPHETIC REVELATION OF MANIFESTATIONS OF NEW ANOINTINGS IN THE END TIME SEASON

This verbatim report is a foretaste of new types of anointing that will be released in the Body of Christ in this season as we have been ushered into the very special moments in the calendar of God in this end time dispensation. God is raising up a new breed of ministers who will move in new types of anointing. The Holy Spirit wants to accomplish great things in the end times, and the way to do this is to release new types of anointing. Great victories shall be accomplished in the realm of the spirit through the release of the new anointings. Presented below is a sevenfold prophetic revelation of manifestations of new anointings in the end time season:

1. THE RELEASE OF NEW WAVES OF THE ANOINTING FOR THE LAST GREATEST REVIVAL

It is undeniably evident that there are new manifestations of the Spirit that are surfacing over the horizon in the Body of Christ in this present time. Such new manifestations heralds the dawn of a new day as we are bring thrust into the very special moments in the calendar of God. Prophetically speaking, a wave of the new anointing shall flood the nations of the world and this shall culminate in the unprecedented stream flow of billions of unbelievers into the Kingdom. Through this Holy Ghost orchestrated invasion of souls, the sound of the abundance of rain which Elijah saw in the spirit realm and then decoded in a prophetic language, shall send signals in the spirit that shall provoke unbelievers to accept the Lord Jesus Christ when this new work begins. The greatest end time revival and spiritual awakening is set forth to break loose as God is preparing His people for an end time supernatural invasion of His glory. However, if Christians do not have fellowship with the Holy Spirit, they may oppose this new move of God and find themselves working against God, just like the Jews did not know God and opposed Jesus Christ when He came in their midst.

2. THE MANIFESTATION OF GREATER ANOINTING & THE FALL OF MANTLES

In this end time season, many great men of God who are serving God today will retire soon and this Holy Ghost divine orchestrated move shall pave a way of for new anointing and mantles to fall upon the new generation. These have been serving God well but under the old types of anointing. Now, the new dispensation calls for new types of anointing. Therefore, the Holy Spirit has to shift them so that a new breed of servants of God will arise with new types of anointing, pick up the fallen mantles and shake the world for Christ and accomplish the last great revival. The Holy Spirit cannot put new wine in old wineskins. The old wineskins will burst and the new wine will be lost, hence the Holy Spirit will have to shift these great men of God first so that they will not be a hindrance to the new anointing which God is unfolding from the Throne Room of Heaven in this critical season. One of the mantles which shall fall upon the masses across the Body of Christ is a mantle of raising the dead under which Smith Wigglesworth, Saint Patrick, Saint Francis Xavier and many others functioned in the past generations.

3. TRANSITION FROM THE REALM OF THE ANOINTING TO THE REALM OF GLORY.

While I have presented a comprehensive topical compendium on the subject of the anointing, it must be understood that the anointing is the second dimension of the supernatural realm. The glory, a higher plane of life in the spirit is the third and highest dimension in God. Therefore, in this end time season, there is an emphasis in the supernatural for a progressive transition from the realm of the anointing to the realm of God's glory. There is a paradigm shift in the governance and administration of the anointing to the release of the glory and for the masses to stride in the deeper territories of the Glory Realm. Through the anointing, many believers shall be catapulted on an expedition, right into the higher realms of God's glory, to explore and discover things they have never experienced before. Increased visitations to the Throne Room shall therefore become a common occurrence in the Body of Christ as the masses are launched into the greater depths of God's presence. The opening of the Heavens to connect man with the rain of new anointing, shall be culminate in many being elevated to greater heights in the supernatural realm.

4. THE UNPRECEDENTED MOVE OF THE HOLY GHOST & THE THICKENING OF THE REALM OF THE MIRACULOUS

In this last dispensation, as the new anointing is increasingly released and precipitated from the Throne Room, the greatest miracles, signs and wonders ever witnessed in the history of the Bible shall be wrought by the hands of the new breed of workers as God launches man in the depths of the realm of the miraculous. We are beginning to feel the sprinkles of this massive global revival sweeping across the Body of Christ as we await His second coming. Metaphorically speaking, we are beginning to experience a whirl of extraordinary divine aura invading the natural realm, leaving the masses dazzled to the last degree. God is exploding in the demonstration of power as the mass are witnessing a factory of mind-blowing signs and wonders, coupled with a warehouse of jaw-dropping miracles, which are culminating in an inventory of breathtaking testimonies, across the globe. As the masses step into the realm of the undefinable, uncharted and unrecorded miracles, signs and wonders in this season, the raising of the dead shall become the order of the day as many will be lifted to the level of their callings. New spiritual experiences and encounters in the supernatural realm will be chronicled as the new breed steps into the realm of new spiritual manifestations such as open trances, open visions and divine transportation in the spirit realm.

5. THE DISPENSATION OF REVELATION

As the new waves of the new anointing blow across the nations, many will be awakened to the reality of fresh revelations of God's word, unearthing and unleashing of hidden mysteries of the Kingdom. As the masses connect themselves to the Word, streams of revelations shall flood their spirit and cause them to fathom deep, raw and undiluted truths and insights. Revelation is what sparks off a renaissance and provokes a spiritual revolution in the natural realm. It grants unrestricted access to the higher realms of glory and the deep things of God. It is revelation that brings elevation in the realm of the spirit. Revelation unlocks destiny, decodes destiny codes and jettisons one into unknown arenas of their manifested destiny. Revelation breeds supernatural acceleration of things in the spirit realm. It produces a breakthrough in the realm of the spirit, which is a sudden burst of advanced knowledge that takes you past a point of defence. It is through revelation that many believers will be catapulted to deeper realms of the Spirit, to do the impossible.

6. A HEIGHTENED DEGREE OF ANGELIC MANIFESTATION AND VISITATION

It is important to note that God is spearheading an end time revival through His angels, hence the angelic era has once again exploded. The release of the overflow anointing shall act as a lubricant in the supernatural realm, to invoke angelic transportation into the natural realm. In this season, the standard of angelic activity shall be heightened as the anointing is catapulted beyond the vicinity of church bars and programmes to spill over to the masses. Manifestation and visitation of angels will no longer be a ministry as angels shall visibly manifest in physical form just like human beings. Angels will no longer be seen in an apparition or expanded form in the spirit realm as has been the norm but they shall be encountered as spirit beings in a physical form. Angels will be physically seen invading churches, the market place, places of business, the streets and the public arena, expediting and enforcing God's end time plans, shortly before He closes the curtain at the end of this age.

7. THE MANIFESTATION OF THE WEALTH OF HEAVEN THROUGH MIRACLE MONEY, GOLD DUST AND OTHER PRECIOUS STONES

There is a new move of God, which marks the greatest prosperity revival ever witnessed in the history of humanity, characterized by the supernatural manifestation of the wealth of Heaven though Miracle money, instantaneous debt cancellation, wealth transfer, financial and food multiplication, a heightened degree of visible angelic manifestations as well as the stirring of a pool of creative miracles in which the original blue print of body parts emerge in bodily territories where they previously did not exist. This third wave of prosperity revival is also coupled with what we call *"the Golden Rain,"* which is the supernatural appearance of Heavenly precious stones such as gold dust, diamonds, silver and supernatural oil on the surface of buildings and in some cases, raining down through the hands and other body parts of believers during worship sessions, where they gather to honor the Lord. This wave has culminated in the rise of Kingdom Millionaires and Billionaires to channel humungous wealth into the Kingdom. This spectacular divine phenomenon has attracted global attention as it has dominated international news headlines, invaded every space on social media and

became a hotly contested topic of discussion in many Christian forums

PRAYER FOR IMPARTATION OF THE ANOINTING

Heavenly Father, in the Name of Jesus Christ, I thank you for the depth of revelations of your Word encapsulated into this writing. I believe your Word and embrace these revelations for my season. I believe that I'm catapulted into the realm of the anointing. I therefore receive an impartation of the overflow anointing from you into my spirit, right now. By faith I believe I have received and now I'm rightly positioned and ready to propagate the world with the anointing of the Holy Ghost. I unapologetically declare that I am the world's most anointed man/woman. I am saturated with high volumes of the anointing, I'm submerged into greater depths of the anointing, and I'm filled to the brink of full capacity with the measureless anointing of the Holy Ghost; my cup runeth over. By reason of the anointing no sickness, darkness, neither evil nor power can stand on my way. As the breaking forth of the waters, so does the anointing upon me breakthrough in every sphere of life. Thank you for making me such a wonder in this world and a miracle worker to launch the world into greater depths of the miraculous. I ascribe unto thee all the glory, Honour and Power due your name.
Amen!!

Congratulations!
And Welcome to the league of The Anointed!

PRAYER FOR SALVATION

If you have never received Jesus Christ as your Lord and Personal saviour, loudly recite the following prayer, now:

Dear Heavenly Father! I present my life before you today. I confess with my mouth that Jesus Christ is Lord and believe in my heart that He died on the cross and was raised from the dead after 3 days, for the remission of my sins. I acknowledge that I'm a sinner and ask you to forgive me for all the sins I have ever committed. Wash me with the precious blood of Jesus Christ and write my name in the Book of life. I therefore receive eternal life into my spirit right now. I declare that from henceforth, Jesus Christ is my Lord and Saviour and I proclaim His Lorship over every area of my life. Thank you Lord Jesus Christ for saving my soul. I'm now a child of God, born again, born of the Spirit of the living God.

Amen!

Congratulations and Welcome to the family of God. You are now a brand new creation that belongs to the lineage of the blessed, the Royal priesthood, the Chosen generation and the highly favoured! Most importantly, you have now received the most precious possession of Heaven, the anointing of the Holy Spirit, glory to Jesus!

AUTHOR'S PROFILE

Frequency Revelator is an apostle, called by God through His grace to minister the Gospel of the Lord Jesus Christ to all the nations of the world. He is a television minister, lecturer and gifted author, whose writings are Holy Ghost breathings that unveil consistent streams of fresh revelations straight from the Throne Room of Heaven. He is the president, founder and vision bearer of Frequency Revelator Ministries (FRM), a worldwide multiracial ministry that encompasses a myriad of movements with divine visions such as Resurrection Embassy (*The Global Church*), Christ Resurrection Movement (CRM) (*a Global movement for raising the dead*), the Global Apostolic & Prophetic Network (GAP) (a *Network of apostles, prophets and fivefold ministers across the globe*), Revival For Southern Africa (REFOSA) (*a Regional power-packed vision for Southern Africa*) and the Global Destiny Publishing House (GDP) (*the Ministry's publishing company*). The primary vision of this global ministry is to propagate the resurrection power of Christ from the Throne Room of Heaven to the extreme ends of the world and to launch the world into the greater depths of the miraculous. It is for this reason that Frequency Revelator Ministries (FRM) drives divergent apostolic and prophetic ministry visions and spiritual programmes such as the Global School of Resurrection (GSR), Global Resurrection Centre (GRC), the Global Healing Centre (GHC), Global School of Miracles, Signs and Wonders (SMSW), Global School of Kingdom Millionaires (SKM), Global Campus Ministry as well as Resurrection Conferences, Seminars and Training Centers. To fulfil its global mandate of soul winning, the ministry spearheads the Heavens' Broadcasting Commission (HBC) on television, a strategic ministerial initiative that broadcasts ministry programmes via the Dead Raising Channel *(a.k.a Resurrection TV)* and other Christian Television networks around the world.

Presiding over a global network of apostolic and prophetic visions, Apostle Frequency Revelator considers universities, colleges, high schools and other centers of learning as critical in fulfilling God's purpose and reaching the world for Christ, especially in this end-time season. As a Signs and Wonders Movement, the ministry hosts training sessions at the Global School of Resurrection (GSR) which includes but not limited to, impartation and activation of the gifts of the Spirit, prophetic declaration and ministration, invocations of open visions, angelic encounters and Throne Room visitations, revelational teachings, coaching and mentorship as well as Holy Ghost ministerial training sessions on how to practically raise the dead. This global ministry is therefore characterized by a deep revelation of God's word accompanied by a practical demonstration of God's power through miracles, signs and wonders manifested in raising cripples from wheel chairs, opening the eyes of the blind, unlocking the speech of the dumb, blasting off the ears of the deaf and raising the dead, as a manifestation of the finished works of the cross by the Lord Jesus Christ. The ministry is also punctuated with a plethora of manifestations of the wealth of Heaven through miracle money, coupled with the golden rain of gold dust, silver stones, supernatural oil and a torrent of creative miracles such as the development of the original blue print of body parts on bodily territories where they previously did not exist, germination of hair on bald heads, weight loss and gain, as well as instantaneous healings from HIV/AIDS, cancer, diabetes and every manner of sickness and disease which doctors have declared as incurable.

The author has written a collection of over **50** anointed books, which include *The Realm of Power to Raise the Dead, How to become a Kingdom Millionaire, Deeper Revelations of The Anointing, Practical Demonstrations of The Anointing, How to Operate in the Realm of the Miraculous, The Realm of Glory, Unveiling the Mystery of Miracle Money, New Revelations of Faith, A Divine Revelation of the Supernatural Realm, The Prophetic Move of the Holy Spirit in the Contemporary Global Arena, The Ministry of Angels in the World Today, Kingdom Spiritual Laws and Principles, Divine Rights and Privileges of a Believer, Keys to Unlocking the Supernatural, The Prophetic Dimension, The Dynamics of God's Word, The Practice of God's Presence, Times of Refreshing and Restoration, The Power of Praying in the Throne Room, Understanding Times And Seasons In God's Calendar, How To Defeat The Spirit Of Witchcraft, The Practice Of God's Presence, 21 Ways Of How To Hear God's Voice Clearly, Miracles, Signs And Wonders, Understanding Prophetic Dreams And Visions, Deeper Revelations Of The Glory Realm, The Prophetic Significance Of Gold Dust, Silver Stones, Diamonds And Other Precious Stones, The Power Of The Apostolic Anointing, Deeper Revelations Of The Five-Fold Ministry, The Anatomy And Physiology Of The Anointing, How To Activate And Fully Exercise The Gifts Of The Spirit, Healing Rains, The Realm Of Love, The Revelation Of Jesus, The Second Coming Of Jesus and Rain of Revelations,* which is a daily devotional concordance comprising a yearly record of 365 fresh revelations straight from the Throne Room of God.

Apostle Frequency Revelator resides in South Africa and he is a graduate of Fort Hare University, where his ministry took off. However, as a global minister, his ministry incorporates prophecy, deliverance and miracle healing crusades in the United Kingdom (UK), Southern Africa,

India, Australia, USA, Canada and a dense network of ministry visions that covers the rest of the world. As a custodian of God's resurrection power, the apostle has been given a divine mandate from Heaven to raise a new breed of Apostles, Prophets, Pastors, Evangelists, Teachers, Kingdom Millionaires and Miracle Workers (*Dead raisers*) who shall propagate the world with the gospel of the Lord Jesus Christ and practically demonstrate His resurrection power through miracles, signs and wonders manifested in raising people from the dead, thereby launching the world in to the greater depths of the miraculous. To that effect, a conducive platform is therefore enacted for global impartation, mentorship, training and equipping ministers of the gospel for the work of ministry. Notable is the realization that the ministry ushers a new wave of signs and wonders that catapults the Body of Christ into higher realms of glory in which raising the dead is a common occurrence and demonstrating the viscosity of the glory of God in a visible and tangible manner is the order of the day. Having been mightily used by God to raise the dead, in this book, Apostle Frequency Revelator presents a practical model of how one can tap into the realm of God's resurrection power to raise the dead, impact the nations of the world and usher an unprecedented avalanche of billions of souls into the Kingdom, Glory to Jesus! May His Name be gloried, praised and honored forever more!

AUTHOR'S CONTACT INFORMATION

To know more about the ministry of Apostle Frequency Revelator, his publications, revelational teachings, global seminars, ministry schools, ministry products and Global missions, contact:

Apostle Frequency Revelator

@ Resurrection Embassy

(The Global Church)

Powered by Christ Resurrection Movement (CRM)

(Contact us in South Africa, United Kingdom, USA, Germany, Canada, Australia, India, Holland & Other nations of the world).

As a Global Vision, The Ministry of Apostle Frequency Revelator is present in all the continents of the World. You may contact us from any part of the world so that we can refer you to the Resident Ministry Pastors and Associates in respective nations. Our offices and those of the ministry's publishing company (Global Destiny Publishing House (GDP House), are ready to dispatch any books requested from any part of the world.

Email:
frequency.revelator@gmail.com

Publisher@globaldestinypublishers.com

Cell phone:

+27622436745

Website:

www.globaldestinypublishers.com

Social Media Contacts:

The Author is also accessible on Social media via Facebook, twitter, instagram, YouTube, and other latest forms of social networks, as Apostle Frequency Revelator. For direct communication with the Apostle, you may invite him on Facebook and read his daily posts. You may also watch Apostle Frequency Revelator on the Dead Raising Channel a.k.a Resurrection TV and other Christian Television channels in your area.

Christian products:

You may also purchase DVDs, CDs, MP3s and possibly order all of the 21 anointed books published by Apostle Frequency Revelator, either as hard cover books or e-books. E-books are available on amazon.com, Baines & Nobles, create space, Kalahari.net and other e-book sites. You may also buy them directly from the author@ www.gdphouse.co.za. You may also request a collection of all powerful, revelational teachings by Apostle Frequency Revelator and we will promptly deliver them to you.

Ministry Networks & Partnerships:

If you want to partner with Apostle Frequency Revelator in executing this Global vision, partnership is available through divergent apostolic and prophetic ministry visions and spiritual programmes such as the Global School of Resurrection (GSR), Christ Resurrection Movement (CRM), Resurrection TV (a.k.a The Dead Raising Channel), the Global Apostolic & Prophetic Network (GAP), Global Resurrection Centre (GRC), the Global Healing Centre (GHC), Global School of Miracles, Signs and Wonders (SMSW), School of Kingdom Millionaires (SKM), Global Campus Ministry and other avenues. By partnering with Apostle Frequency Revelator, you are in a way joining hands with God's vision and thus setting yourself up for a life of increase, acceleration and superabundance.

AUTHOR'S GLOBAL MISSIONS, PARTNERSHIPS & COLLABORATIONS:

If it happens that you are catapulted into the realm of practically demonstrating the anointing following the reading of this book, please share your testimony with Apostle Frequency Revelator at the contacts above, so that you can strengthen other believers' faith in God all around the world. Your testimony will also be included in the next edition of this book.

If you want to invite Apostle Frequency Revelator to your church, city or community to come and spearhead Resurrection Seminars, Conferences, Dead Raising Training Sessions or conduct a Global School of Resurrection (GSR), whether in (Europe, Australia, Canada, USA, South America, Asia or Africa), you are welcome to do so.

If you want to start a Resurrection Centre or establish the Global School of Resurrection (GSR) in your church, city or community under this movement, you are also welcome to do so. We will be more than willing to send Copies of this book to whichever continent you live.

If you want your church or ministry to be part of the Christ Resurrection Movement (CRM) and join the bandwagon of raising the dead all around the world, you are welcome to be part of this Heaven-ordained commission.

If you want more copies of this book so that you can use them in your church for seminars, teachings, conferences, cell groups and global distribution, please don't hesitate to contact Apostle Frequency Revelator so that he can send the copies to whichever continent you are. Upon completion of this book, you may also visit www.amazon.com and under the "Book Review Section," write a brief review, commenting on how this book has impacted your life. This is meant to encourage readership by other believers all around the world.

If you want to donate or give freely to advance this global

vision, you may also do so via our ministry website (www. globaldestinypublishers.com) or contact us at the details provided above. If you need a spiritual covering, impartation or mentorship for your Church or ministry as led by the Holy Spirit, you are welcome to contact us and join the league of dead-raising pastors that we are already mentoring in all continents of the world.

If you have a burning message that you would like to share with the whole world and you would want Apostle Frequency Revelator to help you turn your divine ideas and revelations into script and publish your first book, don't hesitate to contact us and submit a draft of your manuscript at the Global Destiny Publishing House (www.globaldestinypublishers.com). We will thoroughly polish your script and turn it into an amazing book filled with Throne Room revelations that will impact millions across the globe, glory to Jesus!

The Lord Jesus Christ is coming back soon!

Made in the USA
Monee, IL
20 June 2022

98300585R00085